LESSONS
LEARNED
— AND —
CHERISHED

LESSONS LEARNED — AND — CHERISHED

THE TEACHER WHO CHANGED MY LIFE

DEBORAH ROBERTS

ANDSCAPE
LOS ANGELES   NEW YORK

First Edition, May 2023

10 9 8 7 6 5 4 3 2 1

FAC-004510-23076

Printed in the United States of America

This book is set in ITC Caslon 224/Alisha/Paperback 12

Handlettering and Illustration © 2023 by Gia Graham
Designed by Stephanie Sumulong

Library of Congress Cataloging-in-Publication Control Number: 2022051979

ISBN 978-1-368-09505-1

Reinforced binding

www.AndscapeBooks.com

To Mom and Daddy

Contents

INTRODUCTION

Looking back on my school years, I think they were among the happiest and most magical in my life. I still smile when I think of those days, with my two braided pigtails and bangs, walking through the doors of Perry Elementary school, learning the combination to my first metal locker in junior high, playing clarinet in the band, and finally getting that A on a physics test during my sophomore year. I vividly remember that spring in chorus, when we practiced and practiced "Summer Breeze," by Seals & Crofts. To this day I can still smell the honeysuckle in the air and feel the slight summer breeze against my cheek as I stepped into the courtyard after the final bell rang. That image to this day is a happy place for me, much like the song conveys. My memories of those carefree, sunny Georgia afternoons sum up my emotions about school: I felt joyous and hopeful. I now realize that I owe many of those feelings to some of the teachers whose classrooms I was fortunate enough to find myself in. Some were strict and demanding but also kind, helpful, colorful, quirky, and most important, inspiring.

In my adult life, I often have the privilege of giving speeches all over the country about my career as a television journalist and my life as a wife and mother. In all my talks, I find myself reaching back to my formative years highlighting my parents, loving support, and mentioning Mrs. Dorothy Hardy, my long-ago English teacher.

(During sixth grade, I only knew her as Mrs. Hardy. Who knew that teachers even had first names? We certainly didn't in the South, where everyone was addressed as Mr. or Mrs.) Whenever I spoke adoringly of Mrs. Hardy and her influence on me as someone who expected excellence and hard work and inspired me to aim for the stars, I would always notice broad smiles and knowing nods from the audience. Afterward, many people approached me to share nostalgic memories of their own bold, caring, interesting teachers who changed lives, shared valuable lessons, and sparked big dreams. Some even told me their teachers saved their lives.

If you want to get a noncontroversial, feel-good discussion going, ask someone to recall a memorable teacher and get ready for a trip down memory lane that might evoke tears, laughter, or just simply melt your heart. Everyone seems to have a story about a beloved teacher. Sometimes, the story includes a little dose of tough love, but usually you'll find a warm, inspiring story about being valued, encouraged, and seen.

I still break into a grin thinking about the story Oprah Winfrey shared with me about her beloved grade school teacher Mrs. Duncan. Brooke Shields told me about her former college professor who changed the way she saw herself by encouraging her to believe in her own voice. Chef Daniel Boulud recalled the teacher who encouraged him to reach beyond the small French village where he was raised and to dream bigger. Octavia Spencer had trouble naming just one great teacher who sparked her love of learning, but she remembers the one who made her feel important by praising her in front of the class. Over the course of four months, I called, emailed, and bumped into dozens of friends and acquaintances to ask them to share a story about an exceptional teacher. Time after time I found that nearly all of them couldn't stop talking. But what surprised me most was that it wasn't the grades or assignments that took over their emotions; it was *the teacher* who tapped into something they desperately needed at that moment. Some of the experiences were mundane. Some were remarkable. But all of them remain memorable.

There is no shortage of beautiful quotes about good teachers and how they teach more by being who they are than by what they say. The writer Catherine Pulsifer put it beautifully when she said, "a teacher helps others and influences lives forever." Bruce Lee, the famed martial arts guru, describes teachers perfectly: "A teacher is never a giver of truth—he is a guide, a pointer to the truth that each student must find for himself. A good teacher is merely a catalyst."

I've always revered exceptional teachers. As a journalist, I have sat in awe when interviewing selfless teachers who beam while talking about their students or modestly reveal the extra mile they go for them, often buying school supplies themselves or even footing the bill for items their students couldn't afford, as Misty Copeland's teacher once did when she needed new ballet shoes. Of course we all know that many of these generous teachers may be scraping by to pay their own bills; some teachers take on second jobs to make ends meet.

There seems to be an otherworldly aura that envelops passionate teachers, a kind of higher calling that drives them to take on one of the hardest and most important jobs in our world. In my mind, they are classroom warriors, sometimes truly fighting for their students. For hours each day, they stand before our children, some of whom are eager and happy to learn, while others may be dealing with personal challenges, insecurities, or struggles. A trusted teacher may be the only person who can spot a child's ambition, special gift, or even heartache. And sometimes it's that teacher who offers a treasured moment of affirmation, a lifeline, or just a much-needed hug.

Teachers, knowingly or not, build foundations and inspire big hopes and dreams. Some adults credit a teacher for their careers or their positive outlook on life. Sometimes we don't realize the effect that a great teacher has had until years later. When we are faced with a situation and we somehow recall the wise words from that unforgettable instructor. Or maybe we're wading through a difficult challenge and out of the blue recall a long-ago teacher who shared a similar life experience. Teachers leave indelible marks on us all. One of my grade school classmates still remembers this little ditty from Mrs. Hardy: "If you have the audacity to doubt my veracity and insinuate that I would prevaricate, then you have an erroneous conception of my character and are guilty of extemporaneous speaking." I bet she never expected that clever rhyme to tease our vocabulary would be repeated decades later.

When I began writing this book, just after the pandemic, I thought it would be a simple tribute to teachers. Then I started to notice a new and disturbing reality: Each day, there were headlines about school staffing shortages. Sadly, teachers are now leaving their profession in record numbers with tales of frustration, discouragement, burnout, and disappointment. Some even complain of feeling like political pawns as state legislatures change and monitor new school policies. Teachers, who were once among the most revered professionals, are now beleaguered and demoralized after years of pivoting during the pandemic. While many parents finally realized how tough the job really is during our attempts to homeschool, we haven't done enough to honor those who do it full-time and love doing it.

Today, it's our teachers who need inspiration, and it is time to herald them. They are guiding and shaping the young minds who will lead us into the future. Most of us still have the highest regard for the incredible men and women who have chosen a career in the classroom. I know I am thankful every day for those who sparked enthusiasm and dreams in my own children. When I began collecting these stories sometimes there were tears when revisiting that old classroom at a pivotal point in life. Some teachers inspired future CEOs, media titans, world-class chefs, award-winning actors, athletes, musicians, writers, and television journalists. Countless lives have been changed by the passion, encouragement, and hard work of the teachers who have dedicated themselves to this admirable profession, and it's time for them to know the positive impact they've made.

This book is a love letter to teachers everywhere.

Deborah Roberts

Mrs. Hardy—a small gesture of confidence can ignite a lifelong fire in a child

---

When I was a kid growing up in small-town Georgia, the seventh of nine children, I was a bit shy and insecure. It's tough to find your voice in a house full of strong personalities, including a few creative and restless spirits who sometimes challenged my parents and their strict rules. We were also making our way through the fog and uncertainty of desegregation. Georgia had finally accepted the new path of our changing nation, and for the first time children of all races were going to school together. After attending an all-Black school for the first three years of my education, I was now about to sit next to white kids in the fourth grade. Like many of my friends, I had played school at home with my younger siblings, even making tests for them, using purple crayon to make a homemade mimeo machine. I was excited about learning. I felt like a big girl in elementary school. But I wasn't completely confident. I hadn't attended kindergarten like many of my friends. Back then you had to pay for it and with such a large family it was out of reach for my parents. When I took my seat I was convinced that the other kids knew more than I did and understood the lessons better. It didn't occur to me that many of us were equally anxious about reading, writing, adding, and subtracting.

So, when we changed schools midstream to integrate, I was even more nervous. I liked my teachers at the Houston County Training

School. They were mostly women who dressed impeccably and wore stockings, and had coiffed hairdos. The same was true in Perry Elementary School. Only most of the teachers were white. I was surprised by how easily I settled in and enjoyed my new classes. There was some anxiety among all the kids, no doubt. This new landscape could just as well have been on the moon. Still, I was excited to go to school and found myself slowly gaining more confidence.

Then in sixth grade I was assigned to Mrs. Hardy's English class. She was stern and proper and very no-nonsense. She had a neatly cropped head full of gray hair and wore tailored dresses and heels. Her signature look was matching red lipstick and polish on neatly manicured nails. Mrs. Hardy terrified many students. There was no gum chewing in her class, tardiness, or talking out of turn. Any infraction would prompt her to send you out of class to sit in the hallway or to the principal's office if she deemed it serious enough. She demanded proper grammar and taught us to diagram sentences and gave everyone a poetry book of classic writers and assigned poems to be learned and recited before the entire class. Mrs. Hardy rarely smiled and graded papers with a red-ink pen. Red circles on a homework assignment spelled trouble. Usually a bad grade.

One day, after returning our essay papers, Mrs. Hardy complimented my work and told me that I was smart and had potential to go far in life. I was elated. Never had a teacher told me that I was smart or that my future looked bright. Now this strict and demanding teacher had seen something special in me. In ME! Suddenly I was like a blossoming flower that had received a precious watering. Mrs. Hardy believed in me, and now I was beginning to see myself differently. I wanted to write more fluently, speak properly, and ace my spelling tests. I felt seen and valued. It had never occurred to me how empowering it could feel to hear a teacher—someone outside my family—say that you are different and have what it takes to soar. I watched Mrs. Hardy intently and was determined to make good grades and to please her. I basked in the glow of her occasional compliments on my work or someone else's. I also learned the value of hard work and determination.

I didn't know it then, but Mrs. Hardy had lit a fire in me to aspire to excellence. From then on, English became a subject that I excelled at. I was teased for my "proper" speech by some of the kids in my neighborhood, but I didn't care. I now believed that I had something special that would propel me to bigger things in life. By high school I had a confidence that carried me and led me to pursue tougher courses like physics and geometry. I knew that I wanted more in life than many of my friends dreamed of. There were other inspirational teachers along the way, too. They all sparked a feeling of enthusiasm for learning in me. I had discovered what happens when you encounter a good teacher. Being seen and embraced and encouraged is powerful. I am so grateful for those gifts given to me by my teachers. And when I correct my kids' grammar or improper sentence structure in a note or school paper, I think of Mrs. Hardy each time. And I thank her.

Misty Copeland

Trailblazing principal dancer at the American Ballet Theatre,
author, entrepreneur

When someone sees something in you,
you can exceed all expectations

Elizabeth Cantine came to my middle school in San Pedro, California, as the coach of our winning dance team when I was in the seventh grade. My sister was already part of it, and that was the year I decided I wanted to try dancing outside of my bedroom. I auditioned for captain, and I got it, which was a big shock to everyone. Most of the kids had been dancing at school for years, and I wasn't on anyone's radar. For me to just show up and be made captain, everyone was like, "Who is this girl? And why does she think she can audition for this position and get it?"

When I walked into the gym for my audition, I saw a very petite Lebanese woman with a short, curly do sitting behind a desk. She was dressed impeccably and had great fashion sense. I'd eventually learn that Elizabeth paid close attention to details, too, so her clothes were always tailored perfectly. She also considered the "line" of what she was wearing, just like dancers observe their lines in the mirror while working on technique.

For the audition we had to choreograph our own solo as well as learn the group number. At that point the only dancing I had ever seen was on BET, MTV, or VH-1. So I had made up a routine to George Michael's "I Want Your Sex." Looking back, I can see how inappropriate this was! I loved George Michael, and I don't think I understood what the lyrics meant. I was one of the first to audition, and neither of us knew it, but I was giving Elizabeth an introduction to what the next ten years of her life would look like. She could see my potential even with that racy song.

In seventh grade my nickname was "mouse." At four foot eight, I was petite for my age, but I always had the Copeland muscles. Big calves run in my family for sure. I looked like a tiny athlete, but I had never participated in any organized sport. I was this tiny, quiet waif of a thing who could get by without anyone noticing me. I was just the sister of Doug and Eric, the star Copelands of our family. Being a middle child, I was naturally introverted. I was being drowned out by my siblings, who were loud and had big personalities, and I was comfortable in that position. As the fourth of six children, I didn't often get individual attention and I wasn't told I was particularly good at anything. At that time, my family was living in a motel, and it was a low point for us.

Elizabeth was the first person who saw something in me and knew I could do more. I felt like I could tell Elizabeth things and not be judged. She took me under her wing, became my godmother, and has been a big part of my life for decades. She gave me the power to feel like I could rise above my circumstances. She told me, "I see so much potential in you beyond this middle school dance team. I think you should start taking ballet lessons." She introduced me to my first ballet teacher, who was teaching free classes at the Boys and Girls Club. She was helping me out financially when I first started my ballet lessons, and later she and her husband paid for the clothes I needed to dance and pointe shoes, which can be seventy to a hundred dollars a pair. Eventually they built a ballet studio in their house. I'd spend the night there and wake up early on weekends to practice. There were pictures of us all over the studio. This is how Liz is with all her students. She invests in them financially and emotionally, and with her time and love.

My very first performance took place before the actual dance team made their debut at school. Elizabeth had created a solo for me, and I performed it at an assembly on one of the first days of school. The solo was performed to classical music, which I had never heard before. There were hints of ballet technique in that dance, and I think she was testing the waters to see what I could take on. At the end, the auditorium erupted into applause, and for the first time I felt alive and in control. I felt like Elizabeth was giving me this confidence I just didn't have in school. I didn't think I was the smartest, I didn't have tons of friends. I just wanted *to be* . . . but after that solo I wanted to thrive for the first time in my life. This was a huge shift. Dancing was the first time something was mine, and I felt comfortable being able to express myself in a way that made sense to me. I didn't like talking, and I didn't like being the center of attention, so it was a shock to my family that I wanted to go onstage. Stepping into the dance studio and being onstage, I felt serene; this was a new feeling. My mom was on her fourth marriage at that point, and we were always moving to new neighborhoods and new schools. Being onstage or in the studio gave me a sense of control. I had control over my body, and I had control over what I was trying to express. Dance was the thing that pushed me mentally, emotionally, and physically.

Eventually Elizabeth also taught English and history, and she was my sister Lindsay's teacher. As a teacher, Elizabeth is a ball of energy. Every movement of hers is like a performance, even when she's teaching in a classroom. She was always integrating the arts into whatever she was teaching. Elizabeth saw that I had potential to go far, but I don't think either of us knew it would blossom into this. She wanted to give me her experience and knowledge and see where it would take me, like she did for so many other kids.

She's been so proud and is hands-on, yet hasn't been on top of me. She lets me breathe and grow and come back to her when I want to include her or share my appreciation. It's been a very organic relationship, I don't think she knew I would go this far and make history. My ascension was so fast, and she was there for all of it. It's not like she just introduced me to my first ballet teacher and was hands-off for the rest of it. At fourteen I was thrust into the ballet world and called a prodigy. When I did interviews, I always mentioned her, because I wanted her to see the impact she had on me.

Seeing her hold my new son, Jackson, when he was just a few months old made everything come around full circle for me. I know how much of an impact she's had on me, and I wouldn't be here in New York City with the career that I've had if she didn't believe in me. It's mind-blowing. I can't think of a more invested teacher. Because of Elizabeth I understand it's important for my son to have mentors and teachers that are outside of the influence of me and my husband. He needs to have mentors who come from different backgrounds and have different perspectives, so he can see things in a different light than his parents do. The young people and dancers I've mentored myself embrace all different types of mentor relationships. Embrace the different types of mentors that you can have in your life. Acknowledge how much you can gain from someone who has experienced life differently from you.

Christy Turlington Burns

Global maternal health advocate,
founder of Every Mother Counts, mother, model

An empowered teacher creates
empowered students

In 1979, when I was in fifth grade, my family moved from a small town in California to Miami. It was a huge move. Not only were we moving across the entire country, we were moving to a much bigger community. My parents worked at Pan Am, so we traveled and had exposure to the world, but the community I was used to living in was provincial. When we arrived in Miami after driving across the country, my parents and sisters and I stayed in a motel while our house was getting set up. It was a strange way for me to start fifth grade, but things started opening up for me after this move. There were Cuban immigrants, Haitian immigrants, and refugees—much more diversity. I liked being aware of what was happening in the world. This was also when I had my first Black teacher at the Coral Reef School in South Florida. Ms. Dane was attractive and stylish. Her hair was loose, and she always wore earrings and lipstick. She was a feminist who wore pantsuits and everything about her screamed "modern woman" to me. The other fifth-grade teacher was more like Dolly Parton with fluffy hair and colorful twin sets. But when Ms. Dane walked down the hall, she was so cool.

My new school was much more rigorous, and it was hard for me to keep up. I remember asking a classmate on the first day of school when recess was. I was surprised when she responded, "Recess? We don't have recess here." I was used to moving around and playing at school. In California breaks were built into the day. It took me the entire year to get up to speed, and I had some reading and math challenges. There were certain things I wasn't great at, but Ms. Dane never made me feel like I couldn't do those things. She inspired me to get better and encouraged me to take my life experiences and apply them to what I was learning.

Ms. Dane was serious and strict, and didn't let students get away with anything. She would stop what she was doing, turn around, and any misbehavior would immediately stop. She enunciated so clearly, and she was engaging to watch. There was something about the way she spoke that made it impossible to not pay attention. My interest in reading started to grow in her class. I also became interested in science that year and I enjoyed being part of the science fair. I was always one of the taller students, so I sat in the back. I remember we were practicing cursive writing and were doing page after page of it. When she complimented me on my longhand it meant so much. To get a pat on the back from her meant a lot. She also managed to be aware of every single student.

I respected what she was able to do as a woman. She kept such a tight ship. She was so present, clear, and in charge. She was empowered. Ms. D represented change in our country and my life and she enabled me to see women as mentors and leaders. She opened me up to the idea of diversity and made me realize a diverse world is a good world. My class in Florida was more mixed than it was in California, with a large Hispanic population. There was diversity of religions too—Baptist, Catholic, Jewish. I had never been exposed to that kind of diversity, either. I feel lucky to have had her. I wish for everyone to have a teacher who can turn something on. Strangely, teachers are valued less and less. When I was growing up, I knew many people who wanted to be teachers. It was a revered profession. Now teachers are overworked and underpaid, sometimes teaching kids with undiagnosed challenges or in overly crowded classrooms. It makes me sad.

Everything in our lives is a step in the direction of becoming who we are supposed to be. Those transitional and reflective moments are important. Ms. D equipped me to move on. She prepared me for all the other phases of life. I didn't know anything about fashion or modeling then. It's possible she had woken up that part of me because I had never noticed style before. If I could say something to her it would be, *Thank you, Ms. D. You are still the face that I see when I think about teachers who made the most impact on me. For over forty years you're still at the top of my list of women who influenced me. The consistency I had with you was a strong through-line that got me to the next level.*

Oprah Winfrey

Award-winning talk show host, producer, author, and
philanthropist

The greatest gift you can give to anybody
is your full presence

I loved school so much that one of the earliest pictures of me, where I'm certainly no more than three years old, has "school days" written on it. I loved the idea of school so much that I would go with my older cousins. They would just drag me along to classes, and I just loved being in the classroom and being around teaching and learning. And that's why I had a "school days" picture long before I actually started school. My birthday came at a time when I couldn't get into kindergarten quite yet, and this was my savior. It changed my worldview completely.

I was born and raised in apartheid Mississippi. It wasn't just segregation; it was an apartheid lifestyle for Black people, and I was never exposed to that, because I never entered the school system in the South. Now I see this as a great blessing. It was God's guidance and favor in my life that my grandmother became ill and I had to be shipped to Milwaukee, where I started kindergarten in a classroom with kids of different colors and backgrounds.

My grandmother had taught me how to read by reading Bible verses and Easter pieces. I also grew up speaking in the church, so I had a fair amount of understanding of how to actually read, and I knew big words from the Bible—I knew all the books of the Bible, could recite the books of the Bible, and write the books of the Bible by the time I had turned six. I had not been exposed to many kids before, Black or white, because I was living with my grandmother in an isolated rural area in Mississippi.

The very first day of kindergarten, I walked in, and I realized, I do not belong here. I ended up writing a note to my kindergarten teacher, Miss New, saying, *I do not "be long" here. I "no" a lot of big words.* Then I wrote the words I knew: *Jeremiah, Hezekiah, Deuteronomy,* and I threw in *elephant* and *hippopotamus* for good measure. My kindergarten teacher asked, "Who wrote this?" I said, "I did." So, she marches me to the principal's office (this was my one and only time going to the principal's office). The principal also said, "Who wrote this?" and they made me do it again. I did it again and threw in a couple of new Bible verses. I got myself moved to first grade the next day.

Now I was in the first grade and it was not very memorable for me. I already knew how to read, so "See Dick and Jane and Spot" and all that was really boring to me, because I'd been accustomed to reading Bible stories like Daniel and the lions. I spent some time in the first grade then skipped to second grade because I was such a strong reader. I was sent to live with my father in the third grade, and that's when the teaching opened up for me. The summer between the first and third grade I went to Nashville to live with my father. That summer there, my stepmother, Zelma, who really doesn't get enough credit in my life, realized that I was a strong reader, but I knew nothing about math. I didn't know my times tables. My stepmother said, "We've got to get you ready for the third grade." I spent the entire summer learning my times tables with flash cards all the way up to twelve times twelve. It was the most miserable summer of my life. I thought she was the meanest person I ever knew for forcing me to ruin my summer. We spent the entire summer going to the library, taking out library books so

I could learn new vocabulary words to prepare for the third grade. I remember my first big word was "continuity."

When I moved into third grade, I was the number one student. I knew all my times tables, I could read, and I could write essays, because my stepmother had me doing book reports. My teacher, Miss Driver, was the sister-in-law of Mrs. Duncan. Mrs. Duncan, the famous Mrs. Duncan! I read a book called *Honestly, Katie John* because there were no books about Black kids or anything Black. There was nothing that related to me as a young Black girl. Katie John had dark hair and sort of a round nose on the cover, so I thought, I guess this is the closest to me I'm going to get. Miss Driver had given us an assignment to read a book in two weeks and give a book report. I read the book in two days and had my report done before everyone else's.

Miss Driver told Mrs. Duncan about this, and this is the reason I loved Mrs. Duncan so much: She said, "My, my, what a smart, beautiful girl you are. You are so intelligent." It was the first time I felt completely seen. It was also the first time I encountered the concept that I wasn't smart simply because I memorized or comprehended things, but because I have a level of intelligence. There was something in me that was intelligent. I remember thinking, I'm not just smart, *I'm intelligent.* Mrs. Duncan allowed me to fully be myself in that I was not embarrassed about expressing my smartness, and I didn't feel ashamed expressing my smartness around her. In other classes I was a little bit reserved—I thought I was going to be made fun of because my hand was always up. I thought I'd be made fun of on the playground: *That girl thinks she knows so much!* Mrs. Duncan saw something that was deeper than my just reading books. She saw that there was a me in there looking for validation, looking to fill myself up, and to be seen and valued. That's where I felt it; I got that from school.

There was a sweetness, a warmth, and a kindness about Mrs. Duncan. She's one of those teachers who back in the day actually loved their students. Like those special teachers, she saw students as an extension of her work and being, and wanted to implant something within her students that was more than what the curriculum said. I thought she was so kind, and I thought she was pretty, and gracious, and she didn't just think I was smart, she thought I was intelligent. Her seeing that in me made me want to please that person. You want that person who sees you to want to see more of you. She seemed to care about what I was interested in, so I wanted to appear more interesting to her. I felt validated; I felt worthy of my smartness, which is a huge, huge thing to be able to step into it and own it. This happened to me in the fourth grade, and I said for years I looked at Mrs. Duncan and thought, I want to be like that. It's like the Nikki Giovanni poem "Poem for Flora": "she went to Sunday school to hear 'bout nebuchadnezzar the king of the jews and she would listen shadrach, meshach and abednego in the fire . . . all she remembered was that Sheba was Black and comely and she would think i want to be like that." It was like that for me, watching Mrs. Duncan every day, the way she was so kind and gracious and yet she was our teacher.

This was in an era where teachers were revered. I remember seeing her in a supermarket, and it was like, Oh my God, she goes to the grocery store? She has on regular-people clothes and tennis shoes! Teachers were like mythical figures to me. I don't know what I thought they did, but I didn't think they went to the grocery store.

In seventh grade I had Mr. Eugene Abrahams at Lincoln Junior High and High School (they were together). He was a social studies teacher who used to come and sit with me in the cafeteria because I was that kid who would always be reading. Sitting by myself in the cafeteria reading among the noise and all the other kids. Mr. Abrahams once said to me, "You're not like the other students. I'm going to get you a scholarship to another school." He got me to Nicolet High School out in the suburbs of Milwaukee, where I was one of two Black kids at the school. I now recognize that while I had no problems with the other children and I could keep up socially, I couldn't keep up financially. I never had money to do the extra-curricular things; I never had money for pizza after school. I never had the ability to socialize with kids beyond the classrooms or clubs after school. This began a downward spiral. I loved being *in* school more than being *out* of school. I disliked summer because I loved the discipline, and I missed being valued and being seen. This is what I've learned from my thousands of shows and interviews— everybody is looking for the same thing: to be seen, to be heard, and to know that they matter. School is the place I felt I most mattered, not with my mother, father, or my stepmother. My stepmother and my father were working middle-class folks, but I still felt that there was a distance there. There wasn't a real connection. I felt connected, valued, heard, seen, important, and worthy in school.

Without school I don't know who I would have been. What makes me cry is that every teacher has the potential to *do that* for a student, make them feel connected, valued, and worthy. Every teacher has the potential, and when you're doing it, you don't even know you're doing it. You do it by your *being*. What I love and remember about my teachers was their *beingness*. It's not like I can remember a lesson I was taught where I said, Oh, I got that! Or something was said, and I thought, Oh, I'll remember that! It's the beingness of them that I remember; it's their presence. The greatest gift you can give to anybody in your life is your full presence. Having a teacher who sees you, and makes you feel that you are the most important student they have, and then they're able to do that with the next student, and the next. That is the gift. That is the gift of teaching and of being. There is no better offering. That's all you have. It's that "I am here, I see you, I hear you, I feel you, and what you say matters to me."

The greatest, *greatest* teacher for me was and has been the *Oprah* show. It allowed me, by listening to stories of thousands of other people to reflect on the story of my own life. With every person, in every interview you think, I've felt that, too, or I didn't experience that, but I know someone who did. It was a great lesson because I talked to many dysfunctional people, and you're saying I don't want to make that mistake, or Oh, I see what the through line is here. I see that these people are not paying attention to their lives, they are not listening to the whispers. The whispers show up in your life before the whisper becomes a big brick upside your head. The *Oprah* show became my greatest teacher because it allowed me to reflect upon and give perspective to what had happened to me, and why and how it happened. I spend a lot of time with inner reflection. In 2020 I was writing the book *What Happened to You? Conversations on Trauma, Resilience, and Healing* with Dr. Bruce D. Perry. I was reflecting on my grandmother and having been sent away, and how I felt as a child. This is when I had the *aha* moment. All this time I thought I was being sent away because my grandmother became ill, which is what the picture looked like.

I realized being sent away was divine timing. I was being removed from segregation. I was being removed from a segregated school and what a segregated environment in a classroom would have done to my kind of mind. I was like a sponge; I was taking it all in. I was also highly sensitive, so I could feel what you *weren't* saying as well as what you were saying. If I had been in the classroom where the order of the day was you've got to work twice as hard to beat these white kids, everybody thinks we're not as good as them, I would have taken up that thinking. Instead, I walked into a classroom where my first encounter with other kids of different races was, *Y'all can't read, but I can. I do not belong here, because y'all can't read and are playing with ABC blocks and I'm spelling Deuteronomy and Ecclesiastes!*

The system is broken. It doesn't work. I don't know when it happened. It might have been with the start of teaching to a test. If teachers have to make certain numbers for a school, they lose sight of the individual. They're trying to make a number just like in television and other businesses. It becomes more of a business than a personal engagement to actually teach, help, empower, mold, nurture, and support the student. I don't blame teachers, I blame the system that doesn't allow for many teachers throughout the country to teach the way they want to be able to teach. I don't even know how they're being trained now, but I just know that when I was growing up it was a completely different era. Every single kid thought Mrs. Duncan loved them the most. I felt that my friend Yvonne Thomas, who was in my third-grade class, felt it, too. One of the things I love about Gayle is that she was saying her mother had the ability to make every daughter think that she was favorite daughter. I am who I am because of Mrs. Duncan and all my favorite teachers.

I am who I am because they contributed to the *amness* of me. I mean my teachers truly—Mrs. Duncan and all of my teachers really embodied empowerment for me. I felt stronger, better, more capable, and more willing to be myself, which is the only thing that actually matters, because of teachers who saw my strength, my willingness, and desire to want to be more of myself. So, they saw that in me and were able to nurture me and support me in a way that truly encouraged that. It's being seen that makes you the person that you are, and the reason so many kids show off today or are disruptive and can't function is because they have not felt that. I bow at and to the altar of great teachers. Because without them, I would not be *the who* of who I am.

Brooke Shields

Actress, model, author, and entrepreneur

You don't need permission to express your thoughts and opinions

During my sophomore year at Princeton, I took Professor Uitti's comparative literature class, where we read an English translation of *The Second Sex* by Simone de Beauvoir. One day, he asked me to drop by his office. My heart dropped; I was convinced I had done something wrong and was going to get kicked out of school. When it was time for our meeting, I walked into the quintessential professor's office. The walls were lined with books, classical music was playing, and there was a perfect bowl of apples sitting on his desk (naturally they turned out to be from a local orchard). Professor Uitti looked the part, too. His hair was always a little rumpled and there were hints of a beard on his chin. Wire-rimmed spectacles were perched on his nose, and he wore button-down shirts under cardigan sweaters. His shoes looked just a little orthopedic.

When he registered me standing there he said, "Sit down, Ms. Shields, I have just one question for you." I sat down, feeling nervous about what was going to come next. "Tell me, what do you think about hypotheses?" I didn't even know what this question meant! I was so nervous I felt like I could throw up. When I got the courage to speak, I told him that I loved diving into other people's hypotheses—forming an opinion and talking about them. "That's interesting, and I notice you underline your books." Oh no, was I defacing public property somehow? Was I in trouble for this? Now I was even more convinced I was going to get kicked out of school. "Did someone tell you which parts to underline?" No, I replied, wondering where all this was going.

"Do you underline the entire book?" I swear Professor Uitti's eyes were boring right into my head. I started to feel panicked. "Of course not, just the parts I find interesting or important." He nodded. "Okay, well then, tomorrow in precept I'd like you to raise your hand and talk about something you've underlined." Precept is an open forum where students would share opinions and challenge the opinions of others, and it's a big part of the Princeton experience.

The next day in precept, Professor Uitti asked, "Ms. Shields, did you think anything was important in the chapter we read?" I was ready. I shared a key sentence I had underlined, and this spurred a lively, thematic discussion that took place over the next two hours. As I was leaving class, Professor Uitti stopped me. "Ms. Shields, I'd like you to start having faith in your own hypotheses." This was a defining moment for me, and it permanently changed what I thought about myself, my ideas, and my opinions. What he said resonated. It had never occurred to me to have faith in my own instincts. For most of my life I had been taking other people's directions about what to do, how to feel, where to stand, and how to act. I was in an industry where no one wants you to have opinions, because it can threaten their agenda. It made everyone's lives easier if I *didn't* form opinions. I had never thought to nurture my intellect, and this is not something that is nurtured in the entertainment industry. That day in precept I felt like I was heard for the first time. This small moment resulted in something so much bigger—the knowledge that *what I thought was important* was worth discussing. I had been so afraid of being wrong that I never shared what I thought was important. I just sat back and listened as other people shared their thoughts. I didn't realize that until that moment I felt like I *needed permission* to have an opinion.

I felt emboldened by what Professor Uitti taught me. I ended up majoring in literature. I loved that there was no wrong or right answer, I could have my own opinion. Professor Uitti wasn't telling me to pick the right thing, he was telling me I had a voice. He taught me to ask myself, *Why did this sentence call out to me?* when I was alone with a book and my pen. Since opinions aren't right or wrong, I understood I could have been refuted. But I was freed from needing to listen to the voices of others before I could voice my own. I also understood that people can disagree and there's still a lesson to be learned. I grew up in a world where everything was right or wrong, and I was always expected to be right. Professor Uitti showed me that I was never alone because I could consult this entity that happened to be my psyche. I could go back out into the world and say *I don't think this is right* or *Maybe we should do this instead.* It was incredibly empowering.

At one point during my college career, it was decided I would do a press conference. I matriculated at Princeton after many years in the public eye as a well-known model and actress. For most of my life, I was very recognizable and the press was curious about my transition from model/actress to student. The idea was that if I addressed the press and talked about what my life was like at college, I would be left alone. I felt different at the press conference—bolder and smarter. I imagined the press would be proud: *Look how well Brooke is doing!* I know my answers were more articulate that day, and this took everyone by surprise. They kept asking me the same question over and over, like they were waiting for the old Brooke to answer it. I realized that people didn't want me to be smart or articulate. My being articulate threw them, because I was no longer malleable.

I hear Professor Uitti in my head almost every day. When I start to doubt myself, I can get my confidence back because I have a home base in my own psyche. After I graduated, I'd call him about every role I played. I'd say, "I'm going to play a magazine editor, do you have any ideas?" He'd always pick a story from French literature and say, "You know, that character reminds me of a story from Proust or maybe something from Baudelaire." Of course, neither of those writers was ever a magazine editor, but it was a quality from their stories he was referring to. What he taught me bled into my acting by helping me connect my intellect to my craft. I started doing research for my characters. When I was a kid I said my lines, got in a car, and went home—there was no craft in that. Professor Uitti was a genius. He was so well-read. And he nurtured my intellect in a way no one had done before. I learned that my brain was mine and mine alone, and brain power is something that can never be taken from me. Sometimes I still see my own underlines in my head!

Teachers are overworked. The commitment to care so much for so long must be exhausting. Teachers are invaluable and can impact a young mind whether it's kindergarten or college. I always loved my teachers and wanted their guidance, validation, and approval. These women and men gave me their unconditional support and unconditional love, when that wasn't something I had in the entertainment industry. Now it's time to teach my children that everyone has an opinion, and to ask them, "What do you think of hypotheses?"

Octavia Spencer

Oscar award–winning actress, author, and producer

Reach for the lowest branch on the tallest tree

Teachers have always influenced me. I love educators! The motto of the Montgomery, Alabama, school system is "learn by doing." Every one of us had an abacus on our desk. I loved school so much and was so excited to go that I had perfect attendance from first grade through sixth grade (my mother did not play with missing school). In first grade, life was all about manners. I was barely six, and I'll never forget Ms. Bradford. She was a beautiful woman, like a movie star or Clair Huxtable. "You all need to practice your deportment. You can follow Octavia as an example." I couldn't believe it. *That's me!* It puffed me up. That was also when I learned that school wasn't just about education, but also socializing. And I talked a lot. Another teacher once said, "Octavia is loquacious." I had to run home to look up the meaning of that word. Being loquacious is probably why I once got a B in conduct, and nothing short of an A was accepted in my house when it came to that subject.

Ms. Bradford saw something in me, and she nurtured that curiosity. She told me to "Reach for the lowest branch on the tallest tree." I didn't understand exactly what she meant, but I knew it was about learning and growing, and she helped me grow. I hated reading aloud. I was never diagnosed with a learning disorder, but learning to read was a struggle. And because she knew I hated reading aloud she called on me. This made me more confident to speak up in public; I became more extroverted. I overcorrected my homework and made it into the gifted class, where I would work on mazes and puzzles. I could finish a maze in thirty seconds. I believe children who are dyslexic should be heralded and cheered on—you can't shut down a child in those formative years. You'll hurt their growth. I also wrote a play in Ms. Bradford's class for Black history month. There was only one other person in my play, and I didn't give her any lines.

I've had many wonderful, kind, and nurturing teachers, and they all demanded excellence. Mrs. Holley looked just like Barbara Mandrell. My class was trying to win a pizza party from the March of Dimes, and Mrs. Holley said I could be "the ambassador." She laid the foundation for me to be a leader. Mr. Holbrooke, Ms. Elmore, Miss Head, and my theater teachers Ms. Minter and Ms. Cotton all made an impact on me. A few years ago, after I won an Oscar, Alabama had an Octavia Spencer day, and I got to see Ms. Bradford.

It's important for parents to understand that they need to form a relationship with teachers who are shaping their children. Children probably spend more time with educators than with their own parents. When educators hold these little brains in the palm of their hands, they shape their minds. I think teachers should be paid better, especially with what's happening in schools today. We are asking them to do way too much. I have a couple of sisters who were educators and I hold teachers in very high regard. They play a role that is so fundamentally important in a child's development.

Ann Patchett

Bestselling author and bookstore owner

Teaching someone to read is the most meaningful gift you can give

---

We moved to Nashville from Los Angeles in 1969, arriving on Thanksgiving Day. I was three months into the first grade and five years old. I didn't know how to read. We were living with friends of friends, and just before Christmas I was sent to the Catholic school down the street with my sister and the other little girls who lived in the house. If it sounds like a haphazard arrangement, it was. I found myself in Sister Nena's reading class. What I remember about first grade is that I rarely went to school, and when I did go, Sister Nena was looking for me. For reasons that were entirely her own, she thought it was unacceptable that I didn't know how to read. Sister Nena was child-sized herself, five feet tall and ninety pounds. She terrified me. I hid from her in bathroom stalls and coat closets but she always found me. For the next two and a half years my family repeatedly moved away and moved back. I would think I was done with her but then would turn up in her classroom again. I still didn't know how to read. I was what they used to call "remedial." Sister Nena kept me in from recess through the third grade, eating lunch at her desk while forcing me to sound out words. She believed that the ability to read was non-negotiable. Even though I knew I wanted to be a writer, I didn't want to read, because I couldn't. It was too late and I was too stupid. It was a battle of wills, and in the end the small Italian nun won. She taught me. I resented her terribly for it.

I was forty when we met again. She was seventy-two. She called me because she needed money. She was teaching children to read at a seriously underfunded St. Vincent de Paul school. She asked me to buy books and glue sticks and scissors. She wanted to buy presents for the teachers, who worked so hard for very little. She wanted to give them Lifesavers and little tubes of hand lotion. I took her shopping. We went shopping a lot, and then we started going out to lunch. That was when I finally understood that learning how to read had been important to my life. I say this as a joke but truly, I had never given her credit for her tenacity. She made me read. She would not allow my life to be any other way. Sister Nena is ninety now and one of my closest friends. She calls me Little Ann, and I call her Little nun. I bring her books.

Lucy Liu

Actress, artist, and advocate

A small act of kindness can be a lifeline for a struggling child

---

For middle school I went to IS 145 in Queens. When I reached sixth grade I felt like I didn't quite know what was going on—my birthday is in December, and I was usually the youngest one in the class. We had to choose a language that year, and I picked Spanish. I didn't understand the basics. My Spanish teacher was Mr. Martinez. He had a handsome short haircut, and his hair was swept to the side. He always had his shirt tucked into his slacks and wore a belt; it was like the teacher uniform of that time. One day, he asked me to stay after school so he could help me with my homework, which I had gotten completely wrong—I had been guessing when I filled it out. He sat down with me, and he was the first teacher who ever did this. He wasn't punishing me at all. He took the time to explain that this verb connects to this pronoun. He drew a line from the pronouns to the verbs, and because of his diagram, I could understand it. What he did was simple, but it put me at ease. What he did wasn't that complicated—he just explained it and then created a visual pathway for someone who was obviously struggling to learn. If he hadn't taken that time out of his busy schedule to help me, I never would have understood, and I would have failed Spanish. He plucked me out from being towed under. I was struggling so much, I was completely lost, and he threw me a lifeline. This act of kindness that took thirty or maybe even fifteen minutes stayed with me my entire life.

Mr. Davies, the science teacher, also made an impression on me. He had glasses and a beard and he always wore a collared shirt and a tie. That same teacher uniform! I don't recall ever seeing him in a T-shirt. He didn't just show up and teach, he came in prepared and excited, and he made science class so much fun. I wasn't good at science, but he told stories and I found him engaging. He loved being around his students and he understood how to get our attention. Mr. Davies showed me that teachers can be accessible and fun. He was kind, too. Kindness goes a long way when your parents don't speak the same language as you do, and you don't get help with your homework at home.

I was used to grown-ups being very strict and authoritarian. So grown-ups going out of their way and showing generosity of spirit opened my world. I had learned to speak Chinese first and started school before the age of five, and I felt behind in every way. I was incredibly shy, and I did not participate in class ever. I tried to blend into the background as much as possible. I probably knew more than I thought I did, but I wasn't empowered and didn't have the agency to ask questions. My parents were working so hard and weren't around; we were latch-key kids. I never felt strongly about my own sense of self. These teachers emboldened me to ask more questions. I don't think I would have done that before. I felt like I was actually capable, when before I was just cruising through and hoping for the best. Their engagement with me really corrected my way of seeing the world. I always remembered these teachers. It's not like they mentored me through my life or went through a difficult time with me; all they did was show me very simple acts of kindness.

A few years later, in high school, I had a teacher who got me to love math, and it was all because of the way he taught. Everyone was terrified of him! He was strict but not mean; he just expected more because he saw potential in us. I learned so much because of him. There was something about the way he taught that challenged me and made me want to be better. It's a rare quality. Engagement is an important factor to how we absorb things as kids. When something is fun, my son wants to engage! Spur someone's interest by taking something that seems boring and making it magical. The magic makes everything that much more delicious. Turning a boring subject into something that is mesmerizing is a unique talent and a gift to children.

It doesn't take a lot of time to change somebody's life. You can open a pathway for a child by taking just fifteen to thirty minutes to ask, Is there something here that I can help you understand better? This makes them feel like they matter, and they're not being left on the side of the road. It is powerful and impactful if someone takes a moment in their day to really reach out, especially to a child. This is why I love working with children as a UNICEF ambassador. UNICEF engages with kids from all over the world, and you see there is a purity and innocence to these children.

Education is the key to solving many of the issues we have in the world. The fact that art and culture are being taken away because these programs aren't considered necessary is going to be detrimental. All children learn differently, and when you take the creative process away, it limits the way a child can think. We must recognize that there needs to be a balance. Someone might end up being a mathematician, work in computer science, or be a historian, but the point is that you need your mind to expand and contract to have it pulse and be creative. It's kind of like saying playing sports or having kids be active in the park or at recess isn't important. That's not true. There is evidence and research that directly links the vestibular system of a baby to reading and the development of the brain. When babies are on the ground and they're lying on their bellies doing tummy time, which some babies really hate, what they're really doing is learning to scan the room when they move their head around, and that, in turn, is about reading. Giving babies things to sit in is not helpful to them. It's safer, but if they move around, they develop their vestibular system, which is directly connected to their brain stem, and so continues to grow the brain. The brain grows in different ways with different stimulation, so physical activity is crucial to how we learn.

What teachers do is heroic. Your childhood years are a formative time. You are blasted off and rocketed into your teenage years, adulthood, the life choices you make, the friends you have, and the relationships you are in. Teaching is a commitment to being involved in that journey. The commitment can be moment to moment—it doesn't have to be one big event. It doesn't have to be a mission or a charity event. Small moments can really impact a person. A little encouragement can elevate a child in more ways than you would think and launch them into the future. And that's why education needs to be such a priority. I am where I am now in my career and in my role as a parent and as a friend because of Mr. Martinez and Mr. Davies. I don't know where those teachers are, or if they are still at that school. I think about them all the time. How many scientists came out of Mr. Davies's class because he made it so fun? How many people are fluent in Spanish or at least got through the class understanding what it means to connect a pronoun to a verb, because of Mr. Martinez?

Tonya Lewis Lee

Filmmaker, entrepreneur, and advocate

If a teacher sets the bar high, students will be inspired to jump over it

In third grade I went to school in Montclair, New Jersey, and my teacher was Mrs. Moody. She was a young, stylish, articulate, and slender Black woman with cocoa-colored skin, and I wanted to be just like her. She was my teacher, but there was also room for friendship. When I was in school, we'd walk home for lunch, and one day I invited her to have lunch at my home. She accepted and had lunch at my house with me and my mother a couple of times, and we developed a real relationship. Mrs. Moody was the first person to say, "Oh, you are really smart. Yeah, there's something here. You have gifts and talents, and you need to nurture them and take yourself seriously." She saw me as a leader, too. It felt like there was nothing I couldn't do, because Mrs. Moody and I would work things out together, whatever it was. I certainly wasn't perfect, so she disciplined me, too. She'd say, "Tonya, what are we doing here?" While I felt special, she also made sure I understood that while I was smart and worthy, I wasn't any better than anyone else.

Halfway through the school year we left New Jersey and moved to Milwaukee, Wisconsin, where I would have the opposite experience. I was one of two Black children, and I was the only Black child in my grade. Everyone was surprised that I was on the same level as the other students. It was made clear my presence wasn't welcome, that no one wanted me there. I was repeatedly called the N-word by a classmate, and when I brought it up to my teacher, she did nothing about it. In this new school it was all about sitting down and being quiet. It was so devastating to be there and think, This is how we communicate in school here? I had come from such a warm, nurturing place, and I held on tightly to what Mrs. Moody had instilled in me. The foundation she gave me helped me through. In a way, I was grateful for this experience, because now I saw the injustices in the world. It was the beginning of my understanding of racial inequities in the country, which I was seeing firsthand.

During my junior year of high school, we moved to St. Louis, Missouri, where I would encounter another phenomenal teacher, my French teacher, Mrs. Larson. I was good at French. She appreciated that, and she got me to work harder. She encouraged me to travel to France with her and the rest of the group that was going, and we did an exchange program for three years under her guidance. She was a teacher, but also a friend who talked about real stuff. She saw me as a young woman, and she wanted something good for me. After I went to college, I had other French teachers who also set the bar high. They also saw something in me, urged me to work hard, and had big expectations about what I could do.

Whenever I've had teachers like Mrs. Moody, I wanted to perform well and exceed their expectations of me. All these years later I still hold her in such reverence and I'm so grateful. Not too long ago I was working on a project, and I didn't realize it immediately, but I used Moody for a character's name! You don't realize how even a few months learning from someone can make an impression on your life. I also think it's important as Black people to be able to have teachers that look like us as well as inspire us. I'm not saying this always has to be the case! Mrs. Larson was white. But having someone who looks like you can be important.

Teachers are critical and they make an impact one way or another. They can inspire a young person, or they can turn them off learning.

Setting the bar high is important, and tough love is good—but *love* is important. Teaching is a powerful profession, and it needs to be taken seriously. I know it's hard for teachers now, because they don't get enough support, and that's not right. It's one of *the most* important professions.

To this day I still think about the wonderful teachers I've had including Mrs. Moody and Mrs. Larson. If I were able to say something to them, I would say, thank you for being a teacher. You taught me much more about reading and writing legibly, and you taught me the importance of how I present myself. It's a full-spectrum thing—reading, writing, and how you present yourself to the rest of the world. Thank you for seeing me and inspiring me. Thank you for filling up my tank at a young age so that I had a strong foundation to fall back on when I did enter some treacherous waters.

Spike Lee
Storyteller

The right teacher can change your life

It was the fall of my junior year at Morehouse College, and I still hadn't declared a major. Since Morehouse didn't have a film major, I decided to do mass communications, which was film, television, radio, and print journalism. That's where I met Dr. Herb Eichelberger. He was a classic professor, a Black man with glasses and a beard.

A friend of mine got a Super 8 camera and a box of Super 8 film from her dad, and she gave it to me—she didn't want anything to do with it. She was going to be a doctor, and she's a doctor now. It was the summer of 1977, and New York State was *broke*. There were no summer jobs, so I just spent the whole summer running around New York City with my Super 8 camera. I shot a lot of footage from the blackout that darkened most of the city for 25 hours. It was also the first summer that disco hit New York City, and there was David Berkowitz, and it was the summer of Sam. I told Dr. Eichelberger about this, and he said, "Why don't you make a documentary?" I spent the whole fall semester working on it. Dr. Eichelberger was only working three days a week, but he would come in on his days off to open up the lab for me so I could edit. He was encouraging me to work on it all the time. He liked my footage. I showed it to him first and then the rest of the class, and they liked it, too. The film was eventually titled *Last Hustle in Brooklyn*. It was kind of a pun, since the disco craze was going on in New York and everyone was doing the hustle. It was also a nod to the Bertolucci film *Last Tango in Paris* with Marlon Brando, but not the same subject matter at all. I think Dr. Eichelberger saw my potential, but he made all of us understand that this is a very hard profession; things are stacked up against us and we'd have to work for everything. He'd talk long and hard about work ethic.

Dr. Eichelberger was instrumental in my becoming a filmmaker by encouraging me. He had confidence in me, and then I had confidence in myself. It's not like it is now; we're talking about the fall of 1977. There was Gordon Parks with *Shaft*, and his son did *Super Fly*. There was Ossie Davis, and there was some Black independent cinema, but not really any well-known contemporary Black directors. There was Michael Schultz, who really gets lost in the sauce. He was directing all those big-budget films for Richard Pryor when Richard Pryor was the biggest star in Hollywood. He also directed *Cooley High,* one of my favorite films.

I gave Dr. E his due right from the beginning, because he was the one who told me I needed to further my education and made me think about applying to graduate film school. I applied to the University of Southern California and the American Film Institute, but you had to have astronomical scores on the GRE, and I didn't get that. Thank God there are more forward-thinking people at the NYU graduate film school, where you don't have to take a standardized test. I just had to submit a creative portfolio and write an essay, and I got in. After finishing Morehouse in 1979 I came home to go to NYU film school. I finished NYU in 1982, shot *She's Gotta Have It* in 1985, and it came out in 1986.

Because of what I've gone through, I understand the hardships that Black, brown, and poor folks face. If you go to a bad school—and I'm talking about starting in pre-K, we're not even talking about high school—I'm not saying it's a death sentence, but it's rough, and now even more so if you're not born in the right zip code. If you're in the wrong school, you're not going to have the teachers, the facilities, and the technology. Think about the pandemic. In the New York City school system, there weren't enough books to teach kids remotely, and if they had iPads and live in what we used to call the projects, those brick walls are so thick, and you're not going to have Wi-Fi. We still don't know the devastating effect it's going to have on young people who missed two years of school. It's horrible, it's tragic. I come from a long line of educators. My grandmother, who lived until she was a hundred years old, taught art. My mother was a teacher; she taught at St. Anne's in Brooklyn. My father taught bass. I'm a teacher—I'm a tenured professor of film at the NYU graduate film school, and I've been there for twenty years. I'm also the artistic director.

It's really criminal that teachers don't make the money they should or get enough support. And the teachers today, they've really got to want to teach, because they're not going to make any money. It's a profession you choose because you want to help people. You want to broaden horizons and motivate and inspire the young. They talk about doctors, but I'm going to put teachers up there, too. It's a noble profession, and that's why I've been teaching for two decades and will continue to do so. I know the impact that can be made firsthand. I've seen that light in a student's eye, and *I know* I've made an impact. I'm not only teaching at NYU, but on set. There are a lot of people I've worked with who are now in the film industry working in front of and behind the camera. It's a falsehood that teaching only happens in a schoolroom—class can be anywhere. The right teacher can change your life.

Robin Roberts

Anchor of ABC's *Good Morning America*,
producer, and author

Resting on your laurels can only take you so far

When I was in eighth grade at Nichols Junior High in Biloxi, Mississippi, I started hanging out with the "cool kids." I was tired of being the good girl, and I was acting up a bit. My earth science teacher, Victoria Beck, wasn't having it. She came up to me and said, "Nothing from nothing leaves nothing, and you've gotta have something if you want to be in class with me." She was paraphrasing Billy Preston's hit song, and she made her point. She shut that behavior right down. I straightened up after that (also, she knew my parents). Miss Beck was a no-nonsense teacher who demanded excellence. She didn't care who you were; all that mattered was that you were a student, and you were going to do the work. She wasn't handing out gold stars, either. You had to earn everything, and she made you appreciate the work and the fact that you did the work. Kids loved and respected her, and I know she got the most out of me.

Miss Beck wasn't the first teacher who made me want to work hard. At Jeff Davis Elementary School I had Coach Steve Burns for physical education. Every year Coach Burns would choose a winner for the PE student of the year award. I wanted that award so badly. I didn't get it until sixth grade. Fourth grade and fifth grade go by, no award. I knew I was a good athlete, and sixth grade was my last chance to win before moving on to middle school. That year my mom was planning on pulling me out of school a few days early to visit my grandma Sally in Ohio. When Coach Burns heard this, he called my mother and said, "Robin doesn't know this, but she's going to be PE student of the year. Can you hold off on leaving a little longer?" I was thrilled that I had earned that award. There was a side lesson here. Mom flew to Grandma's first, and I flew out a few days later. It was the first time I had flown on my own. Mom said when she saw me walking through the terminal that I looked like I knew where I was going. That trip was a confidence builder because I learned that I could manage traveling all on my own.

Later in life I became good friends with Coach Burns, and he admitted I could have won that award sooner. He wanted to give it to other students who needed it more than I did, and he didn't want me to rest on my laurels. If I had won earlier, I might have leaned on the fact that I was a good athlete and wouldn't have worked as hard. Coach Burns made me earn it. I did wonder at times, Am I a good enough athlete? Why haven't I won? That's when I started to apply myself in the classroom. I was shocked when I learned I was salutatorian of my graduating class; I thought I was being punked. I credit Coach Burns with that achievement as well. He taught me that I can't just rely on my athletic ability to get ahead.

The ripple effect some teachers have can be powerful. I remember my mother talking about her third-grade teacher, Miss Wilma Schnegg, who was the enrichment teacher. Mom recalled that she'd stand in the hall as the kids walked in and would give them each a hug. She suspected it would be the only hug of the day for many of those kids. My mother's parents did not go to school past the fifth and sixth grades, and when it was time for my mother to think about college, they didn't know how to make that happen. Miss Schnegg helped my mother write an essay that landed her a scholarship to Howard University. She was the first person in her family to go to college. All four of her children would go to college as well. Miss

Schnegg stayed in touch with my mom and when she needed more money to stay in school, Miss Schnegg helped my mother plan a recital to raise money. The impact that teacher had on my family was huge.

My mom and dad laid a strong foundation for me, and my teachers reinforced it. When another person echoes what your parents want for you, it reinforces everything. I'm concerned about teachers today. I hope that parents who homeschooled their kids during the pandemic gained a better appreciation of what teachers do. It breaks my heart that teachers are not paid better and more respected and that education is not a field others want to get into. I got so excited recently—Angela Lang from Iowa, who follows me on social is from a long line of educators, and she is thrilled that her daughter wants to be a teacher. You don't hear that much, that people want to make teaching their profession. It's not a job you fall back on or something you do until you find something else. I'm hopeful that a young person will read this book and hear these stories and want to go into education. Teachers have really shaped so many of us and they truly have a chance to impact children's lives.

I am the confident woman I am today because of Victoria Beck. She exuded confidence, commanded it. I also believe I am more intentional today because of her. I am more aware of my abilities beyond athleticism because of Coach Burns. I felt seen, heard, and held because of these teachers. When I was a young adult and starting out on my own, I started to rely on these life lessons. It wasn't just my mother and father who prepared me for life—teachers taught me how to figure things out. They set me up for life. So, teachers, don't give up. What you're doing is seeping through to those kids even if you don't know it.

Anna Quindlen

Author, journalist, and columnist

When a teacher tells you who you can be, your world opens up

I am a writer because of teachers, and specifically because of Mother Mary Ephrem, a nun who was my eighth-grade teacher. She was really smart, took no prisoners, and she raised the bar for all of us. I went to a reunion of my eighth-grade class, and even the people she gave a hard time to talked about what a fantastic teacher she was and how much they learned from her. There was a feeling that Mother was fair, and if you brought your A game you would be praised accordingly. Her responses weren't gender specific. She wasn't like other nuns who favored girls or boys or liked students who didn't rock the boat. She was devoted to the task of helping all of us learn things.

My life-altering moment with Mother Mary Ephrem occurred when I walked up to her desk to get a composition I had written. It had an *A* on the top of the paper. Mother Mary Ephrem wore a full habit, and I never saw anything more than her face, with its wire-framed half glasses. She looked at me from above those glasses and said, "Miss Quindlen, you are a writer." Mother was right about everything, so I couldn't argue. If Mother thinks I'm a writer, it must be true! I was good at writing and had gotten a lot of positive feedback from various teachers over the years, but in this moment, I wasn't "good at writing," *I was a writer.* There is something so powerful about being told *who* you are, by the person who in your mind is the most powerful person in your life after your parents.

As a Catholic girl at a Catholic school in the mid-1960s, I had been trained to fold my hands and follow directions. This wasn't a time when women were expected to be insurrectionary or even working. So the idea that as an inveterate reader I could be a writer was powerful. I looked at the shelves full of books and thought, I could be one of them, and that was radical for a young Catholic girl. I think Mother Mary Ephrem herself was kind of radical. She was smart and outspoken, and so sure of herself. In retrospect, I can see her doing anything from running a corporation to being a United States senator. But at that time there were basically two jobs available for a Catholic woman: One was to be the mother of eight or nine children, and the other was to be a nun.

When I think of teachers, I think about the power of what they do. My sister teaches at a high school in San Francisco, and I have been with her when a student she taught ten to fifteen years ago comes up to her and says, "Ms. Quindlen, you are the best teacher I've ever had." Or, "I've never forgotten you." To be able to make people feel so sure of themselves, what could be more powerful? The ability to lift young people up that way, there's nothing like it. A teacher's passion makes this possible. When I was growing up, the options for a young woman if she wanted to work before she got married had expanded from mother and nun to include nursing and teaching (after she was married no one would let her work). So, not everyone who decided to teach had the passion or the calling.

Teachers who have been called to the profession keep going even though they're not paid what they're worth and they don't always receive the respect they deserve. I feel passionately that teachers' salaries should be higher. I once wrote column where I said, if you have a teacher who changed your life, track them down and write them a note. The truth of the matter is teachers stay put while we move on to jobs that are accorded more respect and pay more, even though *it's the teacher* who may be responsible for the fact that we've moved on to those jobs. I never got the opportunity to talk to Mother about this. I eventually learned she had been posted to Rome and had died years ago. I regret that I didn't take the time to circle back and say *You are the reason I'm here.* I've made a point to write and talk about teachers because illuminating the impact they make is my opportunity to pay it forward. I'm not paying it forward in the classroom, but on the occasions when I have taught, I've walked out of the room and thought, That's the hardest job I've ever done. If I walk away mentally while I'm writing for ten minutes, it's fine. Get distracted in a room full of sixteen-year-olds? You're toast.

Coming out of Covid has been the hardest year for teaching life. If we're going to have a vibrant, exciting, well-managed society with a great future, we cannot let teachers fall by the wayside. We have to do everything we can as a society to help support and reward them. Every CEO, anchor person, US senator, judge, and writer could tell you a story about a teacher who made them who they are today. Erase that teacher and you erase that future.

Jenna Bush Hager

News personality, author, journalist; co-host of
TODAY with Hoda and Jenna on NBC, and founder
of the *TODAY* book club *Read with Jenna*

When someone thinks you can, you do

When I was in fifth grade, I transferred from a public school I loved to an all-girls school, and I wasn't prepared academically. It was a challenging time for me; all the girls seemed more worldly and sophisticated, while I was chubby and used humor to mask my insecurities. Academic and social issues were tough for me, and I didn't feel worthy of being there like the other girls, who had been in school together since kindergarten. To make matters worse, learning came more easily for my twin sister. I worried that I wouldn't be able to get the grades my parents expected of me, but thankfully they didn't compare us.

While I struggled with learning, I always loved to tell stories. My fifth-grade teacher, Mrs. Cunningham, pulled me aside one day. "Jenna, you could be a writer. You need to read all the good books because good writers read all the time." No one had ever told me I could be a writer. It made such an impact on me that I went home that day and told my mom all about it. I would hide out behind a chair in my bedroom with a pen and notebook writing because Mrs. Cunningham told me I could. She gave me permission to be creative. She made me *feel* like a writer. She saw something in me, and I felt like I was enough.

Years later I went back to that school to talk about the publication of my first book. Standing in the auditorium speaking to all the young girls, I suddenly had to ask, "Is Mrs. Cunningham here?" There was a collective "awwwww" and all the girls clapped just upon hearing her name. I loved their response; it filled me up. They all understood that twenty years ago she had changed my life. She had retired two years ago, but I felt her presence in the auditorium that day.

One thing that was particularly telling about the impact Mrs. Cunningham had on me was that I went on to become a sixth-grade teacher at a public boarding school in West Baltimore. I never would have become a teacher if I hadn't had Mrs. Cunningham's example to follow. Those years of teaching were some of the happiest of my life. I admit I never really thought of her influence on me as a teacher until now. Teachers really are the cornerstone of our culture, and they hold the keys to our potential. Kids are our future leaders, and teachers play a huge role in creating them. Teachers look into the eyes of their students and tell them . . . *you are enough.* And this is why there is no job that's more important than being a teacher.

Rosie Perez

Actress, choreographer, dancer, and advocate

When a teacher sees you, everything opens up

Growing up, I was in and out of foster care in upstate New York, where I attended the Brinckerhoff Elementary School. Kids made fun of the yellow-blond hair I had at the time, and they would look at me and say, "That's the girl from the home." In fifth grade, I was both introverted and extroverted at school. I never raised my hand or spoke in class, but call me a name and you'd see my other, angry side. One time, a student called me a fink, and I responded by punching him in the face. My teacher, Mr. Kenny, took me into the hallway to talk about it. "Rosie, why did you do that?" I thought it was obvious. "Because he called me a fink!" Mr. Kenny gave me a kind pat. It was just a little bit of affection, but I wasn't used to it, and I moved away. "Well, Rose, I'm sorry; sometimes I'm a fink, too." I couldn't believe it—did an adult just apologize *to me?* I had never heard an adult apologize for anything.

In fifth grade my teacher was Mr. Mackie. He asked us all what we'd like to be called. My family called me Rose, Rosa, or Rosa Maria, which was my full name, and I wanted my teacher to call me Rose. He was the only teacher who ever called me that; I was Rosie to everyone else. Mr. Mackie was the first teacher I encountered who grouped desks together, so it was almost like the students were sitting at a table. I hated this arrangement, because it meant I had to face the other students. I never participated, even when we had show-and-tell. I didn't raise my hand to answer questions, either; I would have preferred a punishment or a low grade to speaking in class. To get out of the classroom, I would ask to go to the bathroom all the time. Mr. Mackie never said anything about it, because he sensed that I was uncomfortable and needed the break. Sometimes when I went to the bathroom to escape I would just dance. Once I was dancing in the hallway and the janitor saw me. He reported back to Mr. Mackie that I was a good dancer.

We were having a birthday celebration in class, complete with a big cake. Mr. Mackie said, "Rose, so I hear you're quite the dancer." My response was sharp. "Who told you that?!" He smiled and said, "I just heard." He put on the song "Dancing Machine" by the Jackson 5 and grabbed my hand. "C'mon, let's dance. I bet you can!" I pulled away from him and he looked at me kindly. "You don't have to dance, but will you be my friend?" This made me so emotional that my eyes welled up with tears. "Well, don't cry!" I sniffled and said, "I'm not crying, I'd rather see *you* dance." Mr. Mackie said that he couldn't dance, and the kids would laugh at him. "How about this? While they're laughing at me, why don't you join in and wow them?" Mr. Mackie kept replaying the same song while he danced awkwardly with some of my other classmates. When a girl who I thought was mean started doing the robot, and badly, I couldn't help myself. I started to dance, and the class was surprised by my good moves. I remember hearing one of the kids say, "Wow, cool . . ." and that's when I started really showing off. When the song ended, Mr. Mackie was clapping, and he told me to take a bow. So I did, my smile stretching from ear to ear.

At the end of the day Mr. Mackie approached me. "Rose, I know you're very smart, but you don't raise your hand. Did you see how everyone looked at you while you were dancing? Didn't that feel good? That's how you'll feel if you raise your hand in class." I shook my head. "I'm not smart." Mr. Mackie looked me right in the eye. "Rose, you are very, very smart." I still had doubts. "But I mess up in grammar and English." I had a speech impediment then, and I couldn't speak Spanish. I didn't know it at the time, but that was because I had experienced trauma and I would freeze up when I spoke. "That's okay. I'll help you. I also hear you swing a mean bat. I want to see that at recess." At recess I hit that ball right out of the park. I ran the bases and Mr. Mackie put me on his shoulders. I felt so important, but I started to cry. "Rose, why are you crying? I bet those are happy tears." I had never heard of happy tears before.

The next day at school was different. I felt confident; I was inspired. I felt like for the first time that I had been seen. Mr. Mackie acknowledged me as a person and kept pushing me to come out of my shell. During the lesson, I raised my hand. Everyone looked at me, and one of the kids actually pointed at me and laughed. I froze up, but I kept my arm in the air. "Attagirl, Rose, you keep your hand up there. Now tell us, what's the answer?" Mr. Mackie didn't make a big thing out of it, but I raised my hand to answer questions for the rest of the school year.

Mr. Mackie lit the spark in me. He was funny, kind, and made everything interesting. I carried all this forward into sixth grade, and it was like I was a different kid. I didn't hesitate to raise my hand, and I didn't hesitate to show off, either. I made friends (including my best friend, who I'm still close with today), my grades soared, and I joined the glee club. Everything just opened up. I wasn't in his class anymore, but he still made a point to check on me. "Rose, has anyone ever told you you're special?" I responded, "Only my aunt." He nodded. "Well, she must be a special woman, and that's why you're a special little girl."

Years later, I got a call out of the blue from one of my old friends from school. "Mr. Mackie lives in Florida, and he wants to talk to you. He saw *Do the Right Thing* and couldn't believe that was little Rose!" I called him up. "May I please speak to Mr. Mackie? This is Little Rose." There was a pause. "No! What are you doing calling *me?*" I started to cry. "I'm calling to thank you because you changed my life." He was crying, too. After I told him what he had done for me he admitted he had no idea that he had made such an impact on me. "Well, maybe you did this for all the weirdos in the class." Now he was laughing. "You weren't a weirdo, but you were slightly off the beaten path."

I am a vibrant person because of Mr. Mackie. He gave me permission to be that goofy girl who danced in the bathroom—he gave me permission to be *me*. Before Mr. Mackie I loved learning but hated school, but he taught me to love it. If it wasn't for this fantastic teacher I could have disappeared, and that would have been fine with me. But deep down I just wanted to be seen, and he saw me. He changed my life by being a caring, loving, and extremely capable teacher. I co-founded the Urban Arts Partnership because I was directly inspired by Mr. Mackie, and education was my ticket out of difficult circumstances. If I hadn't learned to love school, I wouldn't have gone to college (where I met Spike Lee, who cast me in my first movie)—I wouldn't have the career I have today.

Teaching is hard and teachers have been beaten down mentally, emotionally, and unfortunately sometimes physically. In my work with the Urban Arts Partnership I'd hug teachers and tell them how special they are. I wanted them to know that they are needed, and that they shouldn't give up. Kids from disadvantaged families have had fewer opportunities to learn than their peers who live in wealthier neighborhoods. I don't believe where you live should determine how much money is allocated to your schools—fix this issue, and I think you can fix education. Also, pay a teacher as much as you pay a doctor. A doctor has a human's life in their hands; it's why they are well paid. Teachers also have lives in their hands, and their job is stressful and never ending. They deserve to be paid more. Spread the wealth, pay the teachers more, and education will change enormously.

George Stephanopoulos

Anchor of *Good Morning America*, anchor of
This Week with George Stephanopoulos, and author

Independence leads to confidence

When I was in second grade, Mrs. Nachman noticed that I was fidgety, or sometimes was so bored that I'd drift off to sleep in class. She approached me one day at my desk. "You know what? Instead of coming to class, I want you to go to the library, pick out a book, and read it." Kids never get that kind of freedom, and couple that with the trust she put in me, and I felt like I was being given a big vote of confidence. This also came with a bit of a mandate, so I started reading on my own and I have never stopped. Mrs. Nachman helped make reading one of the loves of my life.

Mrs. Nachman was a kindly teacher who had been around forever. She was curious, in charge, and was almost like a distant figure who emerged to encourage students one-on-one. We all want to be seen, and she saw something in me. That a teacher was saying *You've got this, you can do this on your own* just doesn't happen when you're seven. She opened a door, and I've been curious ever since. She taught me that reading is the key to everything else, and that's certainly been true in my academic and professional life.

The pandemic separated teachers from students, and kids have been denied that one-on-one contact. It might be a cliché, but the fact that our teachers have to struggle and fight to do their jobs and provide supplies for their own students breaks my heart. It is such a critical job, and it must be so difficult, and even feel hopeless at times. She died before I had a chance to tell her what an impact she made, but I am a lifelong learner because of Mrs. Nachman.

Gayle King

Co-host of *CBS Mornings* and
editor-at-large for Oprah Daily

One compliment can spark a sense of pride

My father was an electrical engineer who worked for the government. When I was young, my family was sent to Turkey, and that's where I went to school when I was ten. I remember my teacher, Miss Clifton, had short brownish-blond hair and big eyes. She was probably very young, but as I look back with my sixty-something brain vs. my kid brain, she was likely in her late twenties or early thirties. I wrote a story in English class about a soldier coming home from the war and I used the word "bedraggled" to describe him. Miss Clifton asked me where I got that word, and I replied, "From reading." In Turkey no one really had a television, and I was a big reader who went to the library to check out book after book. I remembered the word from something I had read. The teacher asked, "Well, what does it mean?" I said, "Well, it means someone who looks very tired and very messy." She said, "That's true." I think she wanted to make sure I was using the word correctly. I didn't even think it was a big word, I was just trying to complete the assignment and thought this would be a good word to use in the story. I do remember thinking, What other big words could I use?

Mrs. Clifton was the first person who said to me, "Oh, you could be a good writer." I thought it was a nice compliment and I never forgot it. At that moment, I just wanted to get a good grade, especially because I was bad in math. I still hate math. I was raised in a house where I'd come home from school and my dad would ask, "Do you have any homework?" After I told him I didn't, he'd say, "What's six times six?" When I gave him an answer of thirty-one, he'd say, "Yes, you have homework."

When I was a little girl, I could never have imagined that I'd be on TV. In my early television career, I remember thinking it was helpful to know how to write stories. Back in the day we had to write, edit, and produce our own stories. There was the story I covered where I ended up using the word "bedraggled," and thought Miss Clifton would like that. She encouraged me to do better and be better. I was raised in a house where good grades mattered and being respectful of teachers mattered. Once a note got sent home that said, "Dear Mr. and Mrs. King, Gayle is a very bright student, but she is very talkative in class and tends to be disruptive. I brought this to her attention several times and now I'm bringing it to yours." This was not accepted in my house, that my behavior was brought to my attention by a teacher and it hadn't changed.

I don't think people have enough appreciation and respect for what teachers do. I think the pandemic changed that for parents, certainly when they realized what these teachers are doing! And teachers have lives outside of our children! Every parent I know has a new appreciation for teachers. I feel that a lot of kids today mouth off at their teachers, but this was just not done when I was coming up. Kids, teachers are doing Herculean work to make you better! There are some teachers who see something in you that you don't even see in yourself. Miss Clifton's compliment meant a lot to me because I wanted to get good grades. After that, I was always trying to figure out what I could do to be better. What could I do to get the word "Great!!" with big exclamation marks on my paper? It gave me a sense of pride in my work. Teachers are game changers in ways they don't even know about.

Deborah Roberts

A teacher can water the seeds of determination

Perry High School sat just across town not more than a few stop signs from our small junior high school. But by the time I arrived in the mid-'70s it felt like hundreds of miles away from that pig-tailed, insecure little girl who had taken a seat in a newly integrated school system just a few short years before. I was a happy and contented teen who was beginning to swell with confidence and ambition. Mrs. Hardy, my no-nonsense sixth-grade English teacher, had already lit a fire in me in middle school with her high bar for grammar and vocabulary. She had sparked a newfound sense of optimism and expectation. A bit of a perfectionist anyway, I found myself aiming for the top in all kinds of things—even some weekend chores (though cleaning the bathroom wasn't one of them). At the risk of sounding corny, I loved mowing the grass and even doing the laundry. (I'm a Virgo, so maybe it wasn't a stretch.) But I found something gratifying about pushing our manual mowing machine through the Georgia heat on a late summer day and later having a neatly cropped yard to show for it. My brother Ben was more than happy to let me take over his usual chore. I found something invigorating about putting in an effort and seeing the fruits of my labor. I'd like to say that maybe I was born that way, but truthfully, it was my teachers who watered those seeds of determination. I wanted to be the best in anything I took on.

My mother was always encouraging, she found something special in me like she did with all of her kids.

She loved seeing how gung-ho and happy I was to embrace new ideas. In high school, when I read about a recipe for quiche Lorraine, I insisted on trying my hand at baking this fancy French staple for my southern family. Later I discovered chicken cacciatore. Mom loved it! I know some of my sibs thought I was a weird unicorn—a small-town Georgia girl whipping up strange new dinners that no one could pronounce. Now I look back on those memories with a warm smile and a feeling of gratitude for my various teachers who encouraged me to use my imagination, think outside the box, and to not fear failure. The accomplishment I felt in school sparked a life-altering enthusiasm to embrace ambition and curiosity. (Yes, I was a cheerleader.)

During those teen years, I found myself brimming with excitement for the future . . . *my future*. I had grown up in the Deep South with two hard-working parents who weren't afforded the opportunity to finish high school, they each had to quit and work to support their families. I soon realized that they were offering my brothers and sisters and I the dreams they dared not have. My parents had strict rules and insisted on discipline and hard work as a way out of the Jim Crow barriers they had faced. Church on Sundays was a given, along with a library card, and a passbook account in the local Savings and Loan. College was an expectation, though one of my brothers pushed back, choosing a vocational education instead. But it was clear that my parents saw cracks of light in that dark system of segregation they had endured and envisioned more for their children. They nurtured my desire to go to the University of Georgia and to dream of maybe working in television one day. They were proud of my hard work and led me to believe it was the ticket to success. In school my teachers reaffirmed those values.

Darren Walker

President of the Ford Foundation and activist

There is nothing more selfless, generous, and kind than offering oneself in the service of educating others

---

Mrs. Majors was my fourth-grade teacher at Ashbel Smith Elementary school in Baytown, Texas. It was the 1960s, and the school had recently fully integrated. There had been resistance and it was a slow implementation.

Mrs. Majors was a very stylish, thirtysomething white woman with a Marlo Thomas *That Girl* haircut. She took a liking to me because I think I stood out as one of the few Black students in the school. I was the only Black student in her advanced reading class. At the time, I was struggling at home. My mother had remarried and brought us to this community. I was not particularly happy that I had left my Aunt Ida and the warm little town of Ames, Texas, population 1,200. Also, I was very challenged because I was a gay little boy, and coming to terms with that during that time was something that weighed heavily on me.

My home life was volatile, violent, unsettling, and disturbing. I was acting out by being disruptive, being difficult, or belligerent. On this one occasion, I was in the hallway at school and a boy called me a sissy. I slugged him in the face, and he got up and hit me back and we started rolling around on the hard linoleum floor.

I remember the fluorescent lights and seeing the lockers and kids running around. Mrs. Majors grabbed me and pulled me away. She didn't look at the other boy. I was bloody, I was shaking, I was so angry. I was crying, physically decomposing because I was so upset and angry. It was humiliating to be called a sissy. I had kept fighting him because I wanted to humiliate him the way he had humiliated me.

Mrs. Majors pushed me into the boys' room, "Get into there and clean yourself up. I'll be waiting outside for you." My face was a mess. I was crying. I put my head over the sink and started to clean up. When I finished, she was waiting for me. I had my book satchel. "Come with me." I followed her to her classroom. She closed the door and said, "Look at yourself. I'm ashamed of you. I expect so much more of you than this." I said, "He called me a sissy. I hate him and I can't believe this happened." I couldn't sit in my seat I was so angry. She grabbed my shoulders and said, "Calm down. Darren, you have got to understand—little Negro boys like you who do not learn to control themselves, bad things will happen to them. You have to gain self-control. You have to learn how to control your emotions. You must control your anger. If you cannot do this, bad things are going to happen to you." In her own way she was telling me the harsh reality. It was the first time I heard someone say you have to learn self-control. In a society where injustice exists, it is perfectly reasonable to be enraged as a Black person in this country, but she was preparing me for a world that did not always welcome me. She knew that I needed to be fortified. Part of that fortification was developing tactics and strategies for managing feelings of anger and rage. Some people would mistake her telling me that Black boys need to control themselves as racist itself, affirming a racist system. She wasn't affirming a racist system; she was confirming a reality. If she was a racist, she wouldn't have told me this. If she hadn't believed a little Black boy could be successful in the world, she wouldn't have taken the time. She would have sent me to the principal's office. She invested in me. She thought I was capable of doing great things. It was a generous and radical act of kindness. It was an example of what a great teacher can provide. The life lesson helped me as a child but continues to this day to help center me in a world where I often feel anger.

This lesson has stuck with my throughout my life: As a Black gay man navigating university, law school, and education systems that were white. Coming to New York City and facing racism and homophobia on Wall Street, visiting a historic Black church, and moving to Harlem in the '90s. That lesson of self-control is embedded in my psyche as a critical tool and strategy for coping with the things that I see—the things that have happened to me or others that I believe are enraging and deserve anger. I've had to learn to modulate and to be comfortable with having part of that anger be contained. Mrs. Majors was right. There is not and was not room for me to display the kind of anger that for some white adolescents might have simply been excused by *He's a typical rambunctious, tempestuous boy.*

Over time it gave me awareness of how and when to act when confronted by things that I found upsetting or unjust. She gave me a grounding in how to comport myself in high school when I went on to debates, where you learn by engaging with people who you spar with in discourse. I encountered peers in college, particularly Black students at a big white public university, who were often acting out. I found myself giving them that advice.

I still give that advice. Just today I responded to an email from a Black grantee of an organization who was so angry about something. I responded, "Don't let them throw you off your game." She was going to lose it. "Stop, my sister, comport yourself. You're going to get done what you're going to get done, you've got to be smarter than that." Mrs. Majors was foundational to this.

Often people will use their fist and immediately sound off. Even though that was my culture and home life, I built upon the foundational grounding Mrs. Majors gave me. We have to comport ourselves whether the situation is fair or not. We can't focus on whether it's fair or not; we know it's not fair. I am aware and conscious that there is a real price for that. The mental and emotional toll of suppressing this is a price that is paid by many of us. My point has been figuring out where to put that and how to cope with that. It's the reality.

The journey has been part of the reward. The experience of understanding this system and making it work for us. In college I was head of the student union. After this one day of protests and student action that weren't violent or anything, there were still confrontations and ugly words spoken.

As head of the student union I had to preside, and it was my job to help manage with civility rather than an uncivil series of discussions. I found I was lauded for my ability to de-escalate and calm things. The vice president for student affairs said, "Darren, you have an ability to help bring a sense of calm and equanimity in a situation where others were trying to escalate. You were a leader in that moment. This is what great leaders are able to do." Mrs. Majors was in my head. When managing stress and discordant voices in an organization, we engage with grace, respect, and in a way that elevates a conversation. I am who I am because of Mrs. Majors.

There is no higher calling or more honorable service than teaching and education. There is nothing more selfless, generous, and kind than offering oneself in the service of educating others, in preparing young people for the journey of life. Equipping young people with knowledge, character, and qualities that help them grow and develop. Teaching isn't a job, it's a calling. At the center of it is the noble idea of service that is often overlooked in a society corrupted by inequality and the unbridled pursuit of capital. Teachers can feel marginalized in a society like that. Yet that society cannot function without teachers who care, who act in selfless ways to ensure the next generation is prepared and able to be good citizens and honorable people.

Deborah Norville

Television journalist and businesswoman

Curiosity can lead to the answers to big questions

There is no question about which teacher impacted me the most, and I've said this on national television multiple times. It's Mrs. Louise Eddings, my fourth-grade teacher. I got straight As all through school. The only time I got a bad mark was in penmanship. To this day, no one can read my thank-you notes. I was always told "Miss Debbie talks too much." Mrs. Eddings was the best teacher, and she explained everything in an interesting way. She taught me the Dewey Decimal System. I knew 900–990 was where the biographies were found. I literally read that entire section at Brookwood Elementary School because they were so interesting.

Mrs. Eddings was teaching a social studies class and I had so many questions! I kept raising my hand and asking, "How come?" I was *always* asking her "How come?" I was completely interrupting the flow of her lesson. Finally, she said, "You know what, Debbie? That's a very good question. Why don't you go to the library and look it up and do a report so the whole class will know the answer?" I was delighted to be sent to the library, as it was my favorite place in the school. I think I wrote a total of four different reports before I realized that if I just shut up and let Mrs. Eddings do her job and teach the lesson the way she wanted to she'd get to the answer. What I didn't realize at that time was that this is how Mrs. Eddings gave me my career. My job as a journalist is to wonder, and explain complicated things, and tell stories that will lift you up. But it is also my job to find out the facts and then distill them in a way that will make sense and have meaning for others. That's what those reports were meant to do: take the facts and make them understandable for nine-year-old students.

I've been a journalist for over forty years, and it all started because I had a teacher who let me run loose and *encouraged* me to run loose rather than discipline me. She could have sent me to the principal's office or called my mother to set up a parent-teacher conference. Instead of saying "Oh, this kid is driving me crazy," she supported me and nurtured me and sent me to the library to figure things out myself. When she reinforced for me that it's okay to wonder about things, and that I have the skills to find information myself, she put me on a career path.

By the time I got to NBC, I started to think about how a woman like me from a small town in Georgia ended up at such a lofty place. How did this happen? I realized it was Mrs. Eddings. She's the lady who made me feel that it was okay to be curious and to go out there and find the answers to things. I had another teacher in ninth grade, Miss O., who taught us how to write a business letter. She always insisted on a triple fold. This lesson was also invaluable as I started to make connections out in the world.

I am someone who has three generations of teachers in her family. My grandmother taught first grade for forty-four years. My sister Nancy is still teaching. I keep asking her, "Why don't you retire?" She just looks at me and says, "Because I love my kids." Her daughter was also a teacher for a while. This terrible time we've gone through, and the disrespect we've seen toward teachers is ridiculous. For over fifteen years I hosted the Florida Teacher of the Year event that was sponsored by Macy's for the department of education. It was wonderful to see teachers recognized and lauded by their entire state on television. I think we can do better. I'd like to see teachers saluted on a regular basis. We should stop and simply say thank you to these hardworking people who spend hours with our young minds every day.

Al Roker

TODAY Show co-host and author

A good teacher can help you learn how to roll with the punches

---

I went to a Catholic school in the 1960s, St. Catherine of Sienna. It was a white neighborhood transitioning to a Black neighborhood. Most of the teachers were nuns. We had one lay teacher, Mrs. Eleanor Fryer. I had her for fifth grade, and she was the first Black lay teacher in the Brooklyn Diocese. She was well dressed and fair skinned. Her hair was just so, she wore cat eyeglasses, and had a mischievous smile. She was from the deep south of Georgia. Being from New York City, I didn't have any Southern connections. Everything I knew about the South was from *The Andy Griffith Show*.

Mrs. Fryer was exotic in a way, because she had a deep accent, but she was also someone who was striving because she came from a family of educators. She knew Martin Luther King Jr. and Lena Horne, and she wanted to set us up for success. She said some things that probably wouldn't be said today—there was a bit of goading. "Al Roker, you mean to tell me you don't know the answer to the question, you're a fat head!" Comments like this didn't feel upsetting at all. She once said, "You can't see the answers with your four eyes?" (I had glasses). It was done with a wink and a smile; my classmates who I still know agree with me. She did it to everyone. It was a bit of tough love, a gentle push. There was no sense of anger or meanness behind any of the comments. It was more like *C'mon now, you know this!* She wanted excellence from us. I think she knew that as little Black kids, we'd have to work harder.

I felt like the odd man out because I really did love to read. I was good at visual learning. Mrs. Fryer leaned into that for me. I took refuge in it as a nerdy, chubby kid with thick glasses. I was nerd central, not confident about how I looked, but I was confident in the classroom. There was a reading program that she ran. "You like to read, I knew you'd be a reader because you've got those four eyes." I became a voracious reader and improved my vocabulary. I was reading ahead of most of my classmates because she pushed that. What I was reading was easy, so I got nervous when she moved me out of my comfort zone into an area where I didn't know that I could do it. She felt confident I could do it, and then I felt confident I could do it. As I moved forward, she and a couple of other teachers put me in programs that helped "gifted" and "underprivileged" kids. In sixth grade I went to high school and took upper classes over the summer, and by the end of seventh grade they put me into the higher achievement program, which led to a scholarship to Xavier High School.

When I was seventeen and in college at SUNY Oswego, I met Lou O'Donnell, who was the head of the radio/TV program (now it's called Communications). Lou O'Donnell was an old-time broadcaster with a doctorate and was also on *The Magic Toy Shop*, the longest-running kids show in television on the local CBS station.

Lou O'Donnell approached me and three other guys, because the news director asked if there were any college kids who would be able to do the weekend weather. There wasn't much money to pay anyone. We made audition tapes and weather maps. He took the tape to the station and the news director said, "Who is that kid"? And Lou O'Donnell said, "He's one of the most talented kids I've got." He told him I had a quick wit and people didn't find it offensive. I got the weekend weather job. Lou was a mentor. He made sure I had enough independent studies and took classes so that by the time

I got the Monday-Friday weather job I only had to take six credits my senior year and half of it was independent study.

He saw something in me. I knew I could do radio, but never imagined that I could do TV. Lou O'Donnell thought I could do it when I didn't think I could. I was still chunky, starting to go bald, and I was the first Black anchor to sit at the desk in Syracuse, yet he convinced the news director to take a chance on me.

Today everyone is a winner. We're nurturing kids, which is great, but our kids aren't necessarily prepared to be tough when things get a little bumpy. Different people stand out for different things. I was a good student, and even though it wasn't cool, I wore it as a badge of honor. Teachers recognized that I could do hard things. I had to work at it; it didn't come naturally. But Mrs. Fryer helped instill a work ethic. If you're going to succeed you have to work hard and work smarter than everyone else.

I am more fearless and confident because of Mrs. Fryer and Lou O'Donnell. They believed I could do things, so I had to believe it. They both pushed me out of my comfort zone—going on TV was a leap of faith. Doing the weather while I was still in college happened because a teacher who everyone revered believed I could do it. You have to develop a bit of a thick skin, to learn to roll with the punches. I think it's one of those things that is a life skill that we've kind of gotten away from. A teacher who challenges you is helping you rise to an occasion. Teachers are so battered by so much, school boards second-guessing, administrators not supporting them, parents attacking them. Teachers might be afraid to do what they'd like to do for their students. If they were given support and leeway, they would certainly make a difference in these children's lives.

Michael Strahan

Good Morning America host and
professional football Hall of Famer

The world is wide open for you if you work hard

I went to high school at the Manheim Christian Academy in Germany. It was incredibly small; I was in a graduating class of two students. There were maybe fifteen to eighteen kids in the entire school. Ms. Brenda Brewer, a tall, dark-haired sweetheart of a woman, taught me from tenth to twelfth grade. I was a good student. I was teachable, but I was shy. I was the opposite of what people assume I am now. I was quiet, and not the most confident person. I was more of an observer than a person who would be in the forefront of a discussion.

Ms. Brewer was encouraging and kind. In a class of just two she knew how to give enough guidance to motivate you to achieve on your own. She always took the time to help, and she helped me believe I could be a good student. She was gentle and caring, and this made me not want to disappoint her. She encouraged me to try harder and do better; she wanted me to know I was smart enough to do well. She taught me that the world is wide open for me to accomplish whatever I wanted as long as I worked for it. She said I had the tools for it, and that wasn't something I had ever heard before. This came at an important time in my life. I was in more of a shell, unlike the really popular kids. Wanting to do well spread to other areas of my life. I started working out because I wanted to feel proud about my life all around.

When I hit a certain level of success, I knew it wasn't just me who got me there. It takes a village, and I reflected on this when I came to New York. I know she impacted me. She was like a life coach when I needed a life coach. She's a special woman. I am a better human because of Ms. Brewer. I'm better at dealing with people, expressing sympathy, having empathy, and I'm more encouraging. Ms. Brewer showed me that you can have power and still get respect while being kind. I was glad she was being *who she was*, because she got me here.

When you see a great teacher, it's like they were born to encourage, help, and support others. It's so hard, especially in the environment we're in today. The ability to inspire and influence children is the most powerful thing you can have. Teachers are truly molding the future of children in their most vulnerable years. You never know what kind of impact they'll have on a person. Teachers are here to do the lord's work. They aren't paid enough. The job is emotionally taxing and daunting, yet the teachers handle it with grace and joy.

Bobbi Brown

Makeup artist and entrepreneur

Understanding how you learn can set you on the right path

When I was a kid all I ever wanted was to be a teacher and a mother. That was my goal in life, and I've managed to do both, since I'm a teacher of makeup. But when I think about school, what always gets me is that I was never a great student. I wasn't at all interested in the way most teachers taught. I just wasn't a traditional learner, and growing up I thought that I wasn't smart. One year I had a teacher who did things differently. We were learning how a society functions, and instead of telling us what we needed to know, she let us learn by building one. We made physical models with our hands using glue and scissors, and this time I understood what she was trying to teach us. Understanding that I learned differently helped set me up for success later.

I went to two colleges. The first college I went to was the University of Arizona, and it was gigantic. As freshmen, we'd sit in these huge auditoriums and there would be this tiny teacher down below talking to us. I just doodled since there were no iPhones back then. I was bored, and I didn't learn anything, and then I would come home and try to figure out how I was going to pass the tests. I passed everything with Bs and Cs, but I really struggled. I wasn't happy there.

The next time I visited my parents I told my mom I wanted to drop out. She said "You can't, you have to go to school." She looked at me and said, "If today was your birthday and you could do anything you wanted, what would you want to do?" I knew the answer immediately: "Go to Marshall Field's and play with makeup." My mom thought that was a perfect idea. "Why not be a makeup artist as well?" I still didn't want to go back to school. I didn't understand why I wasn't smart. Why could other kids learn algebra and biology so easily when I struggled so much?

While I didn't want to go back to Arizona, I didn't think beauty school was the right match for me, either. My dad told me about Emerson College, which has an interdisciplinary program where you can design your own major. They didn't have makeup as a major, so I sat down with an advisor and looked at the classes I could take, including art, theater, and television. I literally volunteered to do makeup for anything. I did makeup for school plays and films and I made up kids in the dorm. I opened up at Emerson, because there were lots of creative people who weren't traditional thinkers. I graduated with a BFA in theatrical makeup. I also saw that things were possible, and there was a big world out there. The most important lesson that I learned was that *I am smart*; I just learn differently than most people.

After college I moved to New York City to try to become a makeup artist. One day I went to five different places looking for a job. They all said no. I thought the hell with it, I flipped through the yellow pages until I found "makeup" and started making calls to modeling agencies, makeup artists, and the makeup artists union, and made appointments to go in and talk to people. "I'm here. This is what I want to do, so *what should I do*?" I made it my job to fill my calendar with these go-see appointments, hoping someone would give me a job. Eventually someone introduced me to a famous British makeup artist named Linda Mason, who was looking for assistance for fashion shows and classes she taught. She was really different, doing things like splashing makeup on faces. I assisted her for a while, but not because I was a good makeup artist at that time. I was there to be a sponge and learn everything I could. I was there asking, "Do you need a glass of water?" If a brush fell, I grabbed it. I was always there asking, "What can I do?" To quote Yogi Berra, you can observe a lot by just watching. I was this little timid makeup artist, trying pretty little things, and she basically said, *Stand back and just go for it! Throw splashes of color on the face. Try weird things like putting foundation on the lips. Get out of your comfort zone! Don't just do what I do, figure out who you are.* This made me a better makeup artist because I was still "the natural one," since I was known for creating a natural look, but I understood how to do funny, interesting, weird things, and I had confidence to do it.

New York City is expensive, and it wasn't unusual to find that I had spent too much money. I called my dad and said, "I don't know how to budget!" His response was, "Don't figure out how to budget, figure out how you can make more money." I put an ad in the *Village Voice*, and I got a couple of calls about jobs and was doing more makeup. I would go talk to people at magazines and magazine bookers and someone gave me a break. It took a long time, but I landed a *Vogue* cover with Naomi Campbell. At some point I met a woman whose grandson was a media executive. I asked him if I could be the beauty editor on the *Today* show. He responded that they had never had one of those, and from then on, every month I was on TV as Bobbi Brown, beauty editor at the *Today* show. This was a huge launching pad, and it's how I blew up Bobbi Brown Cosmetics. I continued to be the beauty editor for fourteen years.

Teachers have to figure out how to engage students so they can be the best versions of themselves. Teachers are the most underpaid profession, which is a shame and a crime. That teacher from years ago who let us build a society with paper and scissors laid a foundation for me. We all learn differently. I learned it's okay not to know things, it's okay to ask questions and say I don't understand. Then Linda Mason took it further by teaching me it's okay to color outside of the lines. Those teachers figured out how to keep me engaged and it has led me to where I am today.

Martin Cooper

Fashion designer and entrepreneur

When a teacher hits you a ball, hit it back into their court

Sarah Magoffin was my eighth grade science teacher in Columbia, South Carolina. She had a stern look, but that's not who she was. She certainly *didn't play*, which is what we said in the South. Even though science was her area she saw the creativity in me and encouraged it. I was a motivated young kid who was always sketching and wanted to learn about fashion. She made a safe space for me to do that.

I was the black sheep in my family. I come from a family of dentists. Both of my grandfathers were dentists. My father was a dentist, my uncle was a dentist, my older brother is a dentist, and my middle brother is an orthodontist. At home, my father didn't understand why his son was reading *Vogue* magazine. The only way I could communicate with my father was to make dentistry analogies (I could make them with anything). I never felt comfortable as a creative person around my father. My brothers were the sports guys in the family, but my inclination was discovering and learning about new worlds. I knew early on I wanted to live in New York City. We had the *Encyclopedia Britannica* at home, and the *N* volume had a foldout of the island of Manhattan. I memorized the order of the avenues, because I knew that was where I was going to live someday. When I told Ms. Magoffin about my desire to go to New York to study fashion she said, *Go for it, it's there for the taking. Let it rip, do your thing. Whatever you need, I'm here to support you.* She saw me, heard me, and validated me. She gave me the confidence I needed to pursue my passion.

My mother also played a big hand in making my dream a reality. She claims I came out of the womb with a sketch pad and pencil. As a little kid I was sketching complete collections from day into evening. When I was a teenager, a much older cousin who lived in New York City suggested I check out this fashion school called Parsons. I'd never heard of it. Mom said "Great, let's reach out!" We wrote a letter and included some of my sketches. A few months later we got a call from the chair of the fashion department. "We love Martin's work. We'd love for him to attend a college-level summer program here in New York." Mom said "Great!" but then it sunk in. "He's only fourteen!" Mom negotiated this situation for me, and I was able to attend the summer course in fashion design. At Parsons I met a teacher named Marie Essex. Marie had taught some famous designers including Marc Jacobs, Anna Sui, Donna Karan, and Isaac Mizrahi. She was one of the only people who knew how old I really was. She took me under her wing and watched out for me. I was like her surrogate son during my summer at Parsons. When I went back home Marie and I became pen pals and we kept in touch. When it was time to apply to colleges, I only applied to Parsons. I was thrilled when I found out I was accepted.

Energy flows in two ways. Teachers spend so much time and effort putting themselves out there, but the student has to be willing to absorb the information. It's like Sarah Magoffin hit a ball into my court—but I needed to hit it back to her. When a teacher offers something, it's up to the kid to take them up on it. Students shouldn't take what teachers have to offer for granted, they are in your life to help you. It's a tragedy that there is a shortage of teachers; they are a vital part of society. Teachers are the first people to offer knowledge. . . you don't come into this world baked! You have to be nurtured and encouraged to grow. I am the success I thought I could be because of Ms. Magoffin and Marie Essex. They gave me the confidence I needed to pursue my dream. Being accepted, seen, and validated was intoxicating. Marie was in my life until she passed away in 2001. Ms. Magoffin has been gone about twenty years, but sometimes I wish I could snap my fingers and ask her, "What was it you saw in me?"

LaChanze

Tony Award–winning actress, singer, and dancer

Act as if you matter, and people will treat you that way

I grew up in a military family who moved around, and when I was eight years old, we moved to Connecticut. My parents always got me involved in the local cultural arts scene, and I joined the Bowen/Peters School of Dance in New Haven, Connecticut. Dr. Angela Bowen was my dance teacher, and I studied ballet, jazz, African dance, and tap with her. She was a strong, dark-skinned, regal Black woman with a natural, tight afro who was always draped in a flowing African garment. She was a very firm teacher, and all eyes landed on her when she walked into a room.

I was an awkward little Black girl with a Southern accent who wanted to sing and dance everywhere I went. In New Haven, a little Black girl who moved from Florida might as well have been an alien, but I had loads of confidence when it came to performing. Soon after I started dancing with Dr. Bowen, I learned that my confidence hadn't been earned. I was blessed with natural talent, and I loved performing so much that I thought I knew *everything* I needed to know. I was a bright student and a quick learner, and I didn't have to work as hard as my friends. Dr. Bowen saw me slacking off and she set me straight. I was demoted! She put me in the lower class with kids who were a year younger than me. I wasn't in my age group or with any of my friends. This humbled me in a way I will never forget. I was insulted and embarrassed, and I wanted to quit. How dare she demote me; I am LaChanze! I wanted to quit, but my mother wouldn't let me. "Just because your teacher needed to reprimand you doesn't mean you get to quit. You need to learn that you gain success through work and focus, and not just relying on what comes naturally to you." While she wasn't going to let me quit, my mother had showered me with lots of praise over the years. She didn't want me to have my confidence wrecked by the world as a little Black girl. Black people were always at the bottom of the totem pole, so my mother put me on top—and I thought I could do anything. Dr. Bowen taught me that the totem pole is a lot steeper than you think, and that as a young Black girl in the creative world I would have to work hard and really know what I was doing.

I was desperate to get moved back up into my original group. I stretched every night, even sleeping in a position that I thought would stretch me more. I was determined to prove myself and earn my place back. It took a year, but I did it, and I worked hard to be at the top of that group.

This is one of the best lessons I've ever received. Dr. Bowen trained me to be detailed and go through the process. She taught me that it's by going through the steps and putting your mind to something that you find success. I learned about the importance of consistency, tenacity, and having a strong work ethic. After I rejoined the group, we had the privilege of opening for Katherine Dunham, who is considered the matriarch, queen, and mother of Black dance. I was featured in that performance at Carnegie Hall and saw the good things that hard work could bring.

When I got to high school, my English teacher helped me learn proper diction. My Southern accent wasn't as pronounced as some, but it was strong enough that I didn't finish my consonants. She had me walk around the class saying *justs musts busts*—no dropping the *t*'s (we tend to drop the *t*'s in the South). She also forced me to learn Shakespearian phrases, and this piqued my interest in theater. I started articulating so properly that I got teased for it! She also helped me increase my vocabulary, and I started looking for big words so I could impress her.

In college I met Mark Truitt, who would be my voice teacher for years. I always sang—I was Chaka Khan–ing myself—but I didn't have any technique or stamina. The first time he heard me sing he said, "You have gold in your voice, and I want you to understand that while singing feels effortless now, you'll wear it out if you don't sing properly." At our first meeting he handed me two big bottles of bleach. He asked me to hold them and stand with my arms straight out to the side. "I want you to snort." I thought, You want me to what? He explained that when you snort it raises the soft palate. He was teaching me muscle memory, because lifting your soft palate is an important part of singing. When you snort, the soft palate vibrates, and he wanted me to feel that. Holding the bleach took the focus off my body so I could focus harder on my soft palate. I have had longevity in my business because he taught me how to sing without straining my voice.

Many years later, after I made my way to Broadway in the musical *Company*, I got a message that my voice teacher had passed on. I was so upset I couldn't go onstage, but then I heard him—he was laughing. I felt the joy of his presence and I went out onstage and gave one of my best performances knowing he was with me.

As performers we can get outside of ourselves, distracted by what we look like, what the audience thinks, or what our lines are, and all of this can cause anxiety. These teachers gave me the knowledge I needed to trust myself. What I learned from my teachers gave me the confidence to bring my own passion to the role I played in *The Color Purple*. I could bring my own image of *who* Celie was to the character. I was able to be vulnerable as Celie. I was able to think about my own personal relationship with God and bring that to Celie—God was her best friend.

Teachers today are not given the tools they need to share lessons about how to live in the world and be confident. Teachers taught me that I mattered. I learned that it's okay to take up space and that everything about me was valuable. There is much shame that comes with being a Black girl in America, but my teachers instilled the idea in me that there's no need to feel shame about thoughts, ideas, or emotions. I learned that if you act like you don't matter you won't be treated like you matter, so show up for yourself! I think back to Dr. Bowen—she was such a force, owning every room she entered. I picture her in her flowing garments walking around utterly unapologetically—and because of her I can walk proudly anywhere in the world.

Deborah Roberts

A difficult teacher can inspire you to
persevere and believe in yourself

My cousin recently told me during a phone conversation that she's not surprised that I grew up to be a television journalist. She reminded me that as a teen I was typically glued to the evening news with Walter Cronkite every night along with my parents, watching as intrepid reporters, including a few Black ones, broadcast from hot spots like Birmingham, and later Boston, which were embroiled in violent conflicts over integration. I was fascinated by these reporters like Lem Tucker, Connie Chung, and Michele Clark, who didn't look like the typical white men who always seemed to lead the newscasts. They were savvy and sophisticated and calm under pressure as they told the country about the news of the day. Secretly I was thinking that maybe I could do that one day. But I didn't dare say it aloud. Who would think that a little Black girl from Perry, Georgia, would find her way to a position at a major network news organization? Still, when Barbara Walters gained prominence as a female anchor, I found myself dreaming . . . and mimicking her in my bedroom, my hairbrush as my microphone. There was also Deborah Norville, another Georgia girl making her way up the ranks, and Monica Kaufman, a trailblazing and popular Black Atlanta news anchor.

As I made my way through high school and found my confident voice, occasionally speaking at a school or church event, I believed it could happen. And my teachers encouraged me to believe that I was capable of anything. During my first year of ninth grade, I found myself in an AP physics class. I'm not sure why, because I wasn't especially fond of science or math. But I was determined to push myself and I knew it would be great for college. I was soon met with a terrifying whirling dervish of a teacher named Mr. Griffin. He was a short, wiry man with thinning red hair, freckles, and a slight lisp. He also angered quickly and would speak in focused staccato sentences with spittle coming out of his mouth when a student didn't do the homework or seemed to be cavalier about an answer to a question. In short, Mr. Griffin was frightening. After the first week a couple of my friends dropped his class. But I decided to stick it out. There was something intriguing about this hard-charging teacher who demanded top-notch work and focus. Mr. Griffin's homework and tests were difficult. I stayed up late working on assignments. But as the semester went on, I found myself grasping the concepts. Eventually I made a valuable discovery. *If you're willing to take a leap, to give it your all, and do the work, even challenging situations can pay off.* I noticed that Mr. Griffin softened and occasionally even joked with me because he saw that I was intentional. He wasn't quite the dragon everyone whispered about. And I couldn't believe it when I got an A- on an early assignment. I never liked the minus (I'm a perfectionist, remember). But in physics I took it happily. Mr. Griffin, even with the pursed lips and harsh comments, was teaching us all to persevere and believe in ourselves. He would never win an award for the warmest teacher in school, but he certainly left me with a determination to take on hard projects and to expect success even when you feel a bit fearful.

Teachers have a remarkable ability to help you see things and traits that you may not even realize are right in front of you. I was reminded of that recently after our son Nick began college. As many know, Nick has grown up with learning and developmental disabilities. Problem-solving and school assignments take a little extra processing for him. My husband, Al, and I have been open about what it's like to raise and believe in a kid who is dealing with challenges. Fortunately, we have been able to enroll him in some fine schools with teachers who are skilled in bringing out the best in children who learn differently. His grades aren't always straight As, but he always gets comments about his effort. Nick is one of the most ambitious, focused, and intrepid kids I've ever seen. At age five or six, after his older sister enrolled in tae kwon do, he wanted to join, too. And he was determined to get a black belt. It took him four years, but he finally earned it. And we were in tears when, after a grueling endurance test that ran the kids ragged, the instructor called an exhausted Nick to the front of his group and praised him for having the strongest work ethic and the biggest heart in the class. Nick, he said, had EARNED his belt! That lesson fueled him from then on. Nick has taken that fire throughout life. While he's been fortunate to have some very patient and creative teachers, they have always remarked about HIS indomitable spirit. But I'm convinced that his great teachers have sparked it with their encouragement and kindness, two gifts that the most memorable teachers seem to possess.

Not too long ago when my husband and I dropped him off at a small liberal arts school in the northeast, we met with his academic advisor, a former high school teacher. We were immediately put at ease by this warm, sunny woman with a gentle laugh and a light touch. Before anything else, she wanted to know about Nick's personality and how he expresses himself to help her relate to him. And she added, "From what I've observed so far, I see that he has leadership qualities." My heart melted. Leadership qualities! Our Nick. One of his instructors already sees something in him that even he may not have realized just yet. As he leaves the nest, we are grateful that yet again, a teacher is helping to light the way to something magical. I can't wait to see how it unfolds.

Kenneth Cole

Fashion designer and entrepreneur

Your passions can be turned into a job you love

When I was a student at Great Neck North High School, I loved everything about sports, and I was a huge Mets fan. The Mets were about to play in the World Series, and at that time there were no night games. An announcement was made that vendors were needed because the kids who usually sold popcorn and peanuts at day games on weekends would be in school. There was one exception: kids could work as vendors if they got a written note from a teacher.

I went to see the principal of my school and explained what I'd like to do. I knew our principal to be a nice guy, but in retrospect I probably should have been more intimidated. I got decent grades, but I wasn't exactly an academic star who should miss school. I was a B student, and I was more easily inspired outside of the classroom. I did better when I had an educator who was engaging and inspiring, otherwise I was quick to imagine myself anyplace that wasn't school. I didn't know how he would react. I was surprised when he said, "Yes. Absolutely, I think this would be a great cultural experience for you." He wrote me a letter and I got a job selling peanuts at Shea Stadium during the World Series. My parents didn't think it was a great idea, but it was hard to push back since I'd gotten the okay from the head of the school.

I started my new job, and I loved it. On some level I realized I was being paid to watch sports, and this was actually endorsed by my high school principal. He wasn't saying it was okay for me to run off and miss school, but he thought that being fifteen, I had an opportunity in this job to navigate in the adult world. It didn't take long for me to realize that the city kids who were also working at the game were tougher and smoother, but at the end of the day I held my own. I quickly learned I needed to focus clearly on the task at hand. The big lesson I learned here was that it's possible to marry two passions. For me this would turn out to be combining the entrepreneurial urge to make money with the appreciation of sports. I understood that I could make money and do what I love at the same time. Passions and ambitions can be merged and there are other places to achieve other than school. This was a new way of thinking for me.

Teachers have a big platform and play a big role in the lives of their students. Teachers make connections between what kids are learning in school and what they're learning outside the classroom, and this makes a learning experience more meaningful. Kids have access to everything in the world. Teachers provide context to that information by personalizing it and making it relevant. Now when I meet with young people, I tell them we need to make mistakes and learn for ourselves. And most of all, it's important to learn lessons outside of the classroom.

Mellody Hobson

President and co-CEO of Ariel Investments
and part owner of the Denver Broncos

When excellence is the expectation, kids rise to the challenge

---

In grade school my fifth-grade teacher was Miss Falbo. She was a round, dark-haired Italian woman who was barely taller than we were. She was tough, and a complete authoritarian, but she still managed to exude warmth. We knew she had a heart and she looked after us. Miss Falbo was like a parent you didn't want to disappoint. With one look she could express *You know better*. The story I'm about to share may sound extreme, and whenever I tell it people react with shock. But to be clear, I'm not upset about it, because I know this incident changed my life for the positive and pointed me in the right direction.

When we took a test in Miss Falbo's class, we'd hand our paper to our neighbor, who would check the answers. Miss Falbo would read out the names of students in alphabetical order, and whoever corrected that student's test would say the grade out loud. If you did badly on a test, everyone knew it.

There were weekly spelling tests, and if 100 percent of the class got a perfect score, we would all be rewarded with two Girl Scout cookies. In fifth grade, getting two Girl Scout cookies was about the equivalent of someone giving you two million dollars.

It was the day of the spelling test, and I took pride in myself for being prepared. The words we are supposed to spell are read aloud, and one of the words I hear is "troubled." When the test is over, I give my paper to Amy. When it's her turn to tell Miss Falbo my grade I'm stunned to hear "Ninety percent." I'm thinking this is not possible, I knew every word on that test! I'd soon learn what the problem was. I heard "troubled" when the word was "trouble." The bottom line was that I was wrong. Now I am in a *state*. I'm hoping someone else misses a word so I'm not solely responsible for the entire class missing out on cookies. We get to the last kid, Adam, and I hear "One hundred percent!" My heart sinks—I'm going to be destroyed at recess.

Miss Falbo looks at me. "Listen, I've decided today I'm not going to make the entire class suffer because of you. I'm going make you stand in the hallway while the rest of the class eats their Girl Scout cookies." I get up and walk to the door, thinking don't cry don't cry don't cry. I close the door behind me and put my face up to the tiny little window to watch the class eat their cookies. When they were finished, I was invited back into the classroom. I saw no upside in the moment, but that walk to the hallway was early grit. There was something about Miss Falbo. We all knew she was an exceptional teacher. Tough yes, but that was because she had high expectations for all of us. I also believe she knew what she was doing. Sending me out into the hallway was the work of a master teacher—she *knew* I could handle it. That day I told myself I would never feel that way again, and I worked harder as a result. Ultimately Miss Falbo drove me to have a desire for excellence.

Miss Falbo wasn't the only educator who pushed me at that school. When I participated in the declamatory speech contest in sixth grade, I won and was moving on to compete against the twenty-five other schools in our district. I was going to recite "The Creation" by James Weldon Johnson. The principal, Mary E. Shannon, an old-school, rail-thin woman who always wore a perfect twin set, called me into her office. "You're going to represent our school. Until the day of the competition, you'll come to my office at lunch and recite your speech." Every single day for the next month or so, I ate my lunch and waited outside of her office instead of going to recess. She'd come out of her office and make me recite my speech in the hallway. I did this *every day*.

On the day of the speech the contestants were told to draw a number from a hat to determine the order of the participants. When I drew number twenty-five, my eyes started to well up. I couldn't believe I had to go last, but my mom had a different view of this. "Mellody, because you are last everyone is going to remember you! This is lucky, you are golden!" I sat through twenty-four speeches, waiting for my moment. When I got up there to recite my speech, I nailed it. I won the competition for my school. The triumph stayed with me, and it was a huge confidence builder.

Teachers have a dramatic impact. They are part of our intellectual and emotional development, and they are extremely important. Teachers impact a child's sense of self and what they're capable of. Looking back, I see that while my school was rigorous, most importantly, no one put limits on what I could do.

Ava DuVernay

Director, producer, and writer

When you have a great teacher, there is no task you can't figure out

---

Mrs. Dee was a no-nonsense, curvy white woman who favored pants over skirts and dresses. She was the eighth-grade teacher in my Catholic elementary school, the last teacher you'd have at St. Emydius before you left for junior high. Since the time that I was just a kindergarten student there, I was keenly aware that she was the queen of the teachers—or at least she was in my eyes as I watched her confidently commandeer fellow faculty and families.

When I finally became her student in the eighth grade, my awe of her only grew, especially as I realized that she saw potential in me. When I ran for eighth-grade class president and lost, she appointed me second vice president, because she knew how badly I wanted to be on the student council. I remember the moment she made the announcement, feeling so happy that my heart was actually warm inside my chest. I was overjoyed and pledged to myself to never make her regret it—and I kept that promise.

I recall planning the school's big annual fundraising event, called a jog-a-thon. Students would get people to donate a certain amount of money for how many times they could jog around the school-yard. It may sound easy, but it took us two months of planning, and I was the team lead. It was the first time that I ever remember climbing in bed at night and feeling the sensation of exhaustion.

I'd never experienced that kind of mental and physical relief when my head hit the pillow. Through working on this project with Mrs. Dee, I learned how to take methodical steps to realize a goal, how to organize myself and others, how to delegate and supervise, how to report and communicate success and progress, how to acknowledge and pivot from challenges, and how to be a compassionate leader.

All these things I just described are qualities needed to direct feature films. It was only recently that I connected the dots between my career as a filmmaker and the work ethic that I learned from Mrs. Dee. She encouraged me, pushed me positively, and acknowledged my work in ways that feel like they were a flight plan for the wonderful journey that I'm on career-wise.

Like so many teachers, she laid the groundwork that has served me well and allowed me to serve others. My gratitude is massive and endless. Being Mrs. Dee's student was an extraordinary gift. I salute her and every teacher who has made a child feel like the second vice president in charge of the jog-a-thon: Seen. Valued. Encouraged. Loved.

Emma Lovewell

Peloton instructor, author, entrepreneur, and
founder of *Live Learn Lovewell*

A single interaction with a teacher can change the way you view yourself

---

In my sophomore year English class, I got a B. I did fine, but not great. When it was time to pick classes for my junior year, my teacher suggested I take honors English rather than AP English. My guidance counselor agreed. When I told my dad, who is a professional writer, he disagreed (he's admittedly biased). "I think you're a great writer, and you should take AP English. I know one of the teachers. How about I reach out to him?" At the time, I couldn't think of anything more embarrassing, but my dad set up a meeting at school with Mr. Sharkowitz, aka Shark. Dad came along to introduce us, and Shark told us about his curriculum, and he reviewed some of my writing from other classes. "You can totally do this class. You're a good enough writer and you'll do fine. You can let me know if you need help." Against the advice of my previous English teacher and my guidance counselor, I signed up for AP English.

On the first day of school there are about fifteen of us in the class. Shark walks in and doesn't say a thing. He takes out a couple of sock puppets, puts them on his hands, and talks to us using the puppets. His sense of humor is so dry that he had the entire class laughing hysterically. He was the cool teacher who could pull something like this off for a bunch of high school kids. I remember thinking, Oh my God, he is unlike any teacher I've ever had. He gave us a few key pieces of advice that day. Firstly, he never wanted us to use the words "very" or "too" in our writing. He pushed us to be more creative and felt those words were a cop-out—that they truncated the train of thought. He wanted us to build our vocabulary. "If you use the words 'very' or 'too,' I will deduct ten thousand points from your paper. That being said, you can always rewrite it. You can rewrite it one hundred times if you want to."

I loved the class. We read many books and essays, and we'd critically analyze them and develop theories about what the writer meant. I love to *overanalyze*, so I liked discussing why an author used the color red or other bits of symbolism. But the first time I got a paper back the number NEGATIVE 40,000 was written across it in bright red letters. My friends had scores like this, too. We laughed about it, and then rewrote our papers until we got a good grade. Later on, I wrote papers that he praised, and he'd ask me to read them to the entire class, which felt great.

At the end of the year, I took the AP test, and I didn't do well. I wasn't a great test-taker and this embarrassed me. But what Shark taught me about writing went so far beyond that test. I felt prepared and more confident in my writing after taking that class. When I wrote my college essay, Shark asked if he could print it in the school newspaper. I went on to get accepted by multiple universities. I ended up at the University of Massachusetts at Amherst, where we were all required to take English 101. I couldn't believe how easy it was. I had more knowledge than most of the students in that class. Shark's high school English class was much more challenging than my first college English class.

Now as an author, storyteller, and owner of a blog I write all the time. I never thought I'd be good enough or confident enough to write as part of my career, but I can do this because one teacher believed in me when no one else did. I think about what a huge shift in confidence I experienced. Sophomore year I was so insecure about my writing, and the confidence I gained was due to one person. It's amazing how quickly you can change the way you view yourself based on an interaction with an influential person in your life. I am a writer and I believe in my capabilities because of Shark. Now that I own a business and have written my first book, I remember the lessons Shark taught me. I do limit my use of the words "very" and "too," but I'm not afraid to write, because I know I can rewrite anything. Getting started is always the hardest part. How do I want to come across? What should be the first sentence? I know that I just need to get something down on paper to get the words flowing, and it doesn't matter what they are, because I can always make it better.

Daniel Boulud

Award-winning French chef,
restaurateur, and author

When you are encouraged to dream, possibilities can become reality

---

The teacher I remember most is Mrs. Rebol, who was my teacher in the countryside of Lyon at École Scolaire de Saint Pierre de Chandieu. There were five siblings in my family, and she taught all of us. We each had a different experience with her, and none of us forgot her. Mrs. Rebol was the anchor of the school, kind of like the principal. She was a distinguished lady who had an imposing presence. She was prim and proper, and because it was the 1960s, there was a lot of hair spray.

Mrs. Rebol was fair. We didn't dare challenge her. We knew it was important to learn from her, but we also knew that if we misbehaved, she'd report us to our parents. We all had the same curriculum, but she personalized it, so no one had the same experience. She was loved, and she impacted many people in different ways.

Mrs. Rebol took us on excursions: to see an old castle, cathedral, or a medieval village. The field trips always had something to do with history or geography. She talked about our village as well as other places to see in the world, and I knew I wanted more than school. I wasn't an A+ student, and I needed support. I finished school when I was fourteen and went to live with my uncle and do an apprenticeship. I soon started to see the parallels between good teaching and teaching in the kitchen.

I grew up during a different time, and it's hard to compare teachers from the 1960s to the teachers today. My son and daughter both are in school, and I see how important the teachers are. A good teacher has a personal investment and encourages a kid to dream. Mrs. Rebol helped me see that dreams can become a reality.

Kathryn Chenault

Lawyer and philanthropist

Proper communication is important

Mr. Morgan, my English teacher at Woodrow Wilson Senior High in Washington, DC, wore round wire-rimmed glasses, and he had white hair. He was very commanding, sitting on his stool and leaning on a podium, but he was approachable. He spoke softly, his hands folded under his chin, asking the class, "What do you think?" I always felt comfortable in his classroom. He was a stickler for the English language, and I am, too. In first grade I loved the phonetic chart the teachers used, with a picture of a cherry next to a *ch*. If I could find one of those charts, I'd hang it up in my home!

In Mr. Morgan's class I loved diagramming sentences. I liked the order of it, and appreciated that a sentence has a beginning, middle, and end. I knew I wanted to go to law school and would need to write. I have always wished I was a better writer creatively, but knowing how to construct a proper sentence was helpful.

My husband and I were at the U.S. Open, and I corrected the guide who was giving us the tour. He was mangling the English language. I politely asked if I may correct him. "Are you an English teacher or something?" he asked. I responded, "I probably should have been! I'm just a stickler for the language, because I feel like we're losing it." With phones, everything gets shortened, and even I have resorted to emojis. I used to write complete sentences and check them before I pressed send, because I would be so embarrassed if I made a mistake.

My children know that if they don't ask me a question using proper English, I won't answer it. At work I would correct coworkers. "I hope you don't mind, but that's not how you want to say this. I'm doing this for your own good." To this day when I think of Mr. Morgan, I smile.

It's alarming that teachers are leaving the profession. What is going to happen to the young people if we don't have these teachers? Today, teachers are sometimes the teacher and the parent. It's concerning. We need to acknowledge more the value of teachers and demonstrate how we value them.

Kenneth Chenault

Chairman and managing director, General Catalyst; former chairman and CEO, American Express; and business leader

---

Be a king, not a conqueror

In the late 1950s, I went to school in Garden City, Long Island, a working class town. My father met with the superintendent of public schools, who only wanted to talk about vocational programs. After that conversation my dad decided he didn't want his children attending those schools. It was my aunt who told my dad about the Waldorf School, which had been founded by Rudolf Steiner. I was very fortunate that I had the same homeroom teacher, Lee LeCraw, up until eighth grade and she taught several of our core subjects. She was a strict disciplinarian, but she was very warm. My older brother and sister and my younger brother were all good students, but I was initially indifferent when it came to school. Ms. LeCraw told my parents, "There's something really special about this boy, and he's going to amount to something. He'll wake up. Don't be discouraged." I was a mischievous boy, but she didn't categorize me as a troublemaker, and she became my true advocate.

Ms. LeCraw was one of the first individuals aside from my parents who thought that I had leadership qualities. There was a small hill on our playground, and my friends and I used to play king of the mountain there during recess. These were different times, and in this game the objective was to push all the other kids down and be the last one standing. I really liked that game. I always won and I liked being king of the mountain. Ms. LeCraw took me aside after recess one day and said, "There are qualities that are important if you want to be king. What a king does is protect his people, and he has a responsibility. A king can't be alone. You're acting more like a conqueror than a king." I listened carefully to what she was saying. "The other children look up to you, but you're intimidating some of them. That's not the personality I see in you during the day—only when you play this game." It was my first real moment of self-awareness, and one of the most important leadership lessons I've received. Self-awareness is important when it comes to leadership; you have to understand the impact you have on others. That lesson was a real gift, and she continued to emphasize it to me over the years. I didn't necessarily know what it meant to be a leader, but I knew I wanted to be one.

The next teacher who influenced me was Peter Curran, who was a teacher and the principal of my high school. Mr. Curran sat me down my sophomore year and said, "If you continue to apply yourself, the sky is the limit. You can do anything you want to do." He also emphasized accountability: "You've got to make it happen; things won't just fall out of the sky. You have to apply yourself." He thought I should go into politics or business. Outside of coursework he gave me biographies of Frederick Douglass and Winston Churchill. He gave me books about ancient history and current events. Later he actually took me to visit Bowdoin College in Maine, which was his alma mater. He was instrumental in convincing me that Bowdoin College would be the right school for me.

Before I went to college, I only had experienced being in a predominantly white environment in school, however in Hempstead, I lived in a majority Black neighborhood so I learned to toggle back and forth between these two worlds at a very early age. Fortunately, I had teachers like Ms. LeCraw and Mr. Curran who made it a point to encourage me to develop a sense of purpose, and they consistently demonstrated that they had confidence in me and my abilities. Clearly, it was very empowering to have individuals in my life outside of family who emphasized to me that the sky was the limit if I applied myself. These teachers took the time and interest in me, and they *took action*. They made an incredible difference in my life. They had my back and pushed me and encouraged me to be the best I could be. This was incredibly motivating. It wasn't just about getting As; it was about finding a purpose.

Next to parents, teachers make a fundamental difference in a child's life. We need to honor and respect them. We need to start looking at teachers as people who can change lives. Teachers make an incredible impact, but if you feel disrespected or you're stuck in a bureaucracy, it's easy to become dispirited. It was a *teacher* who told me I could be a leader, and it was a *teacher* who taught me that leaders make a positive difference in other people's lives. I can't think of a more important life lesson.

Sheryl Lee Ralph

Emmy Award–winning actress, singer, author, activist, and
star on the ABC television show *Abbott Elementary*

Change happens when you have the courage to ruffle some feathers

---

My dad was a lifelong educator, but he was also a lifelong learner. He was one of the best teachers ever, and how do I quantify that? Every time I put a picture of my dad on social media I'm flooded with emotional notes and texts about how he impacted his students' lives and how they remembered him. It's a great gift, because he wasn't just my father, he had a presence in our household as a teacher. My dad started off as a music teacher and ended up being a Professor of Diversity and Inclusion. It was so fitting that he would be teaching that course at Rockland Community College. My mother taught as well. She taught sewing and design. She was always there at the Girls' Club, and she was my Brownie leader. Both of my parents were natural teachers.

I'll never forget that my dad loved signs. There was one particular sign that he gave me, and it sat right on the piano. It was just a five-letter word, and it has stuck with me my whole life. It said THINK. He would say, "You're not daydreaming, you're thinking." I just loved that. Whenever anything goes wrong, I stop, breathe, and think. When things go right, I stop and think, How can I do this better?

My mother also taught me an important lesson. My mother was an immigrant, and so I'm an immigrant's child. Immigrants were coming to America in the 1950s in the pursuit of the American dream, and my mother believed it was possible to reach that dream. She always instilled the message in me that I was smart, I was beautiful, and I could overcome obstacles. I loved *Superman*, the old black-and-white TV show. I believed I was a *Superwoman*, but then again, my mother always told me I could do anything. I heard this from her over and over, and so I believed it. I was going to be a Superwoman.

Later on, my dad taught in Waterbury, Connecticut. He was a tough teacher, but was always encouraging. He let you know that learning wasn't going to be easy. You had to study, and you had to practice. If you didn't do those things or respect the time of others, you weren't respecting others and you weren't respecting yourself. All these things were so important. I'd ask, "What's wrong with being late every now and then?" He'd look at me and say, "When you're late you're saying I don't respect your time, or my time is more important than yours."

My parents also taught me that as a child of the sixties, I had to be prepared to fight the good fight, because I would face all kinds of things. I was faced with ignorance, and very often it was the ignorance of adults. It can be hard for a child to stand up for themselves when there are adults around saying things like, "Don't aspire so high," which really meant *Do not aspire to greatness because of the color of your skin.* If you didn't receive a kind of girding of the loins from your parents, your church, and people from your community, you might fall victim to somebody else's ignorance. I was *always* ready to fight the good fight because of my parents. My father broke the color line when people were trying to say that a Black man could not teach in a white school system. He rose to great heights when impediments were blocking the way. He overcame those things.

And I'll never forget when my mother was trying to get a job at a cosmetics counter and the store didn't hire her. They hired a friend of hers who wasn't qualified for the job—because she was a white woman. My mother went right down to the store and said, "I know this woman and she is not as qualified as I am." They ended up having to give my mother the job, and it caused quite a lot of consternation. *Who is this immigrant woman up trying to tell us how to run things here?* She taught me not to be afraid to ruffle some feathers. Because sometimes that's how change happens. You might not get the recognition for it, but it doesn't matter, because it must be done.

I prayed for a television show that could make a difference for people and I was given the gift of *Abbott Elementary*. . . and I feel *good* about it. On the show, I play a kindergarten teacher and the kids learn to hold hands, not yell, to walk (okay, to run when it's appropriate). These are basic things you can master—they will help you throughout your whole life. When I speak to teachers' unions, the members tell me how happy they are *to be seen*, and that they're glad my show doesn't sugarcoat the issues that exist in an urban school. Those teachers are dealing with something that is deeply challenging, but they refuse to be beaten down and continue to give their students the best.

I'm just sad that teachers are becoming so discouraged that they're now leaving their jobs in record numbers. They are choosing not to teach and pass on knowledge. They're choosing not to go into debt from student loans for a job where they're not going to find respect. If we let this continue, the country will suffer greatly, because when there is no one to teach, you can't learn things. And when you don't know things, you can't solve problems. You can't think. Critical thinking is important, and I still think about that five-letter word. I think that's why people have little skirmishes and then decide, *Well, just let me shoot you or ram you with my car*. . . because they don't think.

I've always been able to credit both my parents with the lessons they've taught me, and it all helped my career. I also learned from them that teachers need to be encouraged just like everyone else. I think about how often teachers are disrespected. People do not respect the time they put in. During Covid, people finally came to the realization that it was difficult having children with you ten hours a day, and it's hard to get kids to pay attention no matter how old they are. Suddenly people were like, "Oh, I get this teacher thing! I apologize, I should have shown up for that parent-teacher meeting." *Well, yes you should have!* The bottom line is I am *a much better human being* because my parents were teachers. They were perfectly imperfect teachers who took what they had, poured it into me, and taught me to think for myself.

Kim Godwin

President of ABC News and journalist

A teacher's attention can fill a child's soul with goodness

I was bused to Bayside High School in Queens, which was predominately white with hundreds of people of color. When I say bused, I really mean that I either took three different city buses or two city buses with a mile walk in between. Aside from the long bus journey from my home in Jamaica, Queens, I realize now this was a good thing for me. Going to school in a different community, I learned that everyone is just like everybody else. I was raised by a single mother in a tough neighborhood, and as I was growing up, reading was a form of escapism for me. Other kids wanted to run around and play, but no one wanted to talk about books. I was a shy kid who didn't talk much about what I read, but I could imagine the characters coming alive and the scenes unfolding in my mind.

I was fifteen when I entered the twelfth grade, and Sonya Robbins was my English honors teacher. She was an impeccably dressed woman, always in a dress with a cardigan sweater tied neatly around her, and I wanted to dress just like her someday. I fell in love with Shakespeare in her class. I was specifically intrigued by Lady Macbeth. As I read, I could see her in my mind's eye, trying to wash out bloodstains on her hands that weren't real bloodstains. Ms. Robbins was teaching this kid from the hood about metaphors and how to think critically. I became fascinated by what I was reading and was always looking for meaning in the text. Ms. Robbins had a knack for calling on me and pushing me to answer questions I really had to think about. *What does that mean? Can you take that idea and make real-life connections?* I also learned to always be prepared because *I knew* she was going to call on me. We wrote essays in her class as well, and I always wanted to impress her with my perspective on whatever we were reading. That entire school year I couldn't wait to get to her class. It was because of Ms. Robbins that I fell in love with the learning process, and I earned an A in her class.

At the end of my senior year there was an awards ceremony the students were required to attend. There was one award for the best writer. I was sitting in the audience with my mother when suddenly my name was called, and I couldn't believe it! To this day I well up when I think about it—sitting there next to my mom and being so surprised when I heard my name. I remember thinking, I'm a Black kid in a white school and I beat all these people? Really? Something spoke to my spirit at that moment, and said *Kim, you have a gift.* I realized that if Ms. Robbins thinks I'm the best writer, I must be a pretty good writer! My spirit lit up, and I remember thinking, Oh, I'm ready for this college thing!

When I went to college, I was pre-med. I wanted my mom to be proud of me because I was the first person on her side of the family to go to college. When I started freshman chemistry it soon became clear that there was no way I could do these classes for four years. I had no idea what anyone was talking about, and I had no interest in the subject. I walked out of class that day and stood in the middle of the campus. I asked myself, What are you good at? I knew I was good at writing. I spoke well at church, too. Don't journalists write and talk? That's how I got into journalism. I walked right into that journalism building to find out about what classes I could take, and *that's all she wrote.*

I was fortunate to have more than one teacher who really impacted my life. In kindergarten, Ms. Pyes really saw me, and she allowed me to be myself. One day we were coloring a picture of a stoplight. I wanted to do it right, and I was still coloring when it was time to go to recess. All the other kids jumped up, but I wanted to stay. Ms. Pyes said, "That's okay. Go ahead and finish and you can come out and join the class later." She recognized what I needed as an individual. To this day I understand the importance of seeing people *where they are*, and this has informed my management style.

In sixth grade my family moved to a new neighborhood, and that meant a new school. I was still shy and hadn't made any friends yet. My sixth-grade teacher saw my love of reading and said I could take home as many books as I wanted. She eventually gave me a standard New York City reading test and I scored at a twelfth-grade level. That was an early hint that I had a gift, and my teacher helped me feed that gift with reading. I ended up being the valedictorian of my class that year.

The relationship between a teacher and a student is powerful. To have another person look you in the eye and see you is so important! Whether a student comes to school hungry or has walked through snow or heard their parents fight that morning, they are bringing that to school. In tough neighborhoods, kids are seeing and hearing things that other kids don't hear and see—a fight or maybe even gunfire. When a teacher sees a kid trying to learn something and asks a child to share what she's thinking about, that other stuff can be erased. That teacher is pouring goodness into a child's soul, making them feel worthy of attention. It's validating. My teachers brought me out of my shell and got the shy kid talking about books. My teachers engaged me in conversation, helped me learn to prepare, and gave me the confidence to think *I can do anything*. I was taught I was capable, and that it was okay to be me. I learned that I mattered, that I was good at something, and my opinion was valid. I have cherished these simple lessons that I've carried through my life and still use them today. I stand taller because of my teachers, and the little things they did for me that filled my soul with goodness.

Will Reeve

Television personality, reporter, and journalist

A strength can be nurtured into something even stronger

My sixth-grade teacher Bill Barrett made me a better student, better person, and a better citizen of my school society. He was a role model in every way: compassionate, intelligent, disciplined, and fun. He's everything you would hope to become and everything you'd want your children to have in a teacher. He was many things to me at one time: my football coach, lacrosse coach, and my homeroom adviser. I learned a lot from him academically, but he also taught me how to move through the world, and this has stuck with me. I admire him and have tried to emulate the way he treats people and carries himself.

Mr. Barrett had a personal touch. As amazing and nourishing as my home life was, it was abnormal because my dad (who was a well-known actor and advocate) had been paralyzed and in a wheelchair since an accident in 1995. Attendant challenges came along with that. Mr. Barrett made sure to take extra care of me, and not because I necessarily needed it. I was a good kid, and I generally did well in school. I was raised to care about people, act with kindness, and do the right thing. When I was in third or fourth grade I developed some tendencies to bully, probably because I was big and had underlying angst and aggression born out of the uncertainty of my father's health. This may have manifested in my being rambunctious, and I literally took up space. I might have been overwhelming to other kids who were coming into their own. Mr. Barrett gave me space to navigate all this. He urged me to check in with myself, figure out who I was and who I wanted to be, and see what I could become. In sixth grade he encouraged me to run for class president, which I won. He said that I had the ear of my classmates and their respect, and I should channel my energy into whatever the sixth-grade class president does.

My mom was out of town during parents night one year, so my older brother Matthew drove my dad to school. He had met Mr. Barrett before, but my dad came home raving about him, "He's so smart! I saw your project on the Roman Empire. You must have so much fun." My dad was so impressed by him, and I have yet to encounter anyone who didn't admire him and want to be in his presence. Dad also came to football games, a sport Mr. Barrett coached.

Kids are not usually fired up to go to school, but if you knew Mr. Barrett was waiting for you in homeroom, it helped. He made school exciting. He turned it into a fun destination and an engaging place to be. What was really special about him as a leader was that he played to the strengths of the people in his charge. He would double down on a student's best qualities. He challenged our weaknesses and encouraged us to improve, but all while expanding on our strengths. I wasn't great at math or science; I was more of a humanities guy. Instead of letting me hate coming to school because of math, Mr. Barrett made sure I got the work in those classes out of the way and that I met with those teachers. I think the best leaders see the best in folks and allow them the space and freedom to run with those strengths. Mr. Barrett nurtured strengths so they could grow even stronger. He knew what I was good at and encouraged me to be great at it.

When I was finishing eighth grade, my mom was sick in the hospital battling lung cancer, and my father had died not even two years earlier. Mr. Barrett was part of the rotation of people caring for us and dropping off food. But he was also with me during one of the most seismic moments in my life. On March 6, 2006, the students were watching a faculty basketball game. I was messing around with my friends and being cheeky. He motioned to me to come over to him and I thought I was going to get into trouble. "Walk with me." He took me to my classroom to get my bag. As we went outside, he explained that there was a car waiting to take me into New York City because it was time to say good-bye to my mom. She died that night. I've thanked him for that—I'll never forget what he did for me in that moment.

It says something about our relationship that Mr. Barrett was deemed the right person to talk to me and walk me out that day. He kept checking on me and let my family know I should take as much time as I need to process my loss. School could wait. When I missed my friends and wanted to come back, he was there to make sure I could adjust to the emotional and sensory overload. When I went on to high school, he still went out of his way to take me to dinner, just to check in and make sure I was okay.

Like many of his students who are my good friends, I've stayed in touch with him over the years. We have a more adult relationship now; he'll take me for beers in the city. I have been able to tell him directly, multiple times, how sixth grade was my favorite year of school. It's a great pleasure to develop a relationship with a role model, to learn about who they are as people. To see their humanity and complexities and still feel they are worthy of admiration. It's fun to see your heroes as they really are and still think they are heroes. Mr. Barrett is the type of person I'd like to be, and if I have a daughter, I hope she'll marry someone like him. He's a special person, and I'm not alone in this sentiment. Everyone who crossed his path adored him. He took the time to care about each of us, and that doesn't always happen.

I've been so fortunate to have dedicated, tireless teachers. My level of respect for teachers is boundless. Shaping the lives of the next generation is the most essential and difficult job anyone could have. I completely understand those who are just tired. I wish I had an answer to fix these issues. Teachers are not paid well enough, or appreciated enough, and they don't have the right resources. The odds are stacked against them far too heavily.

The Reverend Eva Suarez

Associate rector, St. James Episcopal Church, New York City

Don't be quiet; don't hide yourself

I went to the Duke Ellington School of the Arts in Washington, DC, where I was able to study classical voice. The students were sorted into classes for our voice lessons, and we would stay with that class our entire high school career. My teacher was Mr. Jackson, a tall, elderly Black man who spoke in beautiful cadences and always stood up straight and proud. He was tough and intimidating, and I was nervous the first time I met him. But once I got to know him, it became clear he was a teddy bear. If you *just tried*, he'd love you.

Our voice classes required vulnerability. When it was my class's turn to work on a piece, we'd sing alone, in front of Mr. Jackson and the other students. Sometimes we'd be standing up there for twenty minutes, so there was no hiding if you weren't prepared. One thing he couldn't stand was quiet singing—he'd surprise us by simply yelling "LOUD!" If he knew we were trying or were working on a difficult piece, he didn't hold any mistakes against us, but he'd shout, "If you're going to be wrong, be wrong loud! Don't be quiet, don't hide yourself." He instilled a strong sense of pride in all of us. He always related to us with seriousness and dignity, and he demanded excellence.

I was the only student in my class who wasn't in show choir, so if they had a performance, it meant I had Mr. Jackson all to myself. The texts we used were the classic texts that anyone who has studied classical singing has used. We sang in Italian and German, and we also used Harry T. Burleigh's anthology of spirituals. I approached the spirituals with trepidation. The word "river" was spelled "ribber" to give the song a slave intonation. I told him I felt conflicted about singing this. This launched a long conversation about spirituals, slavery, and faith (he knew how much the church meant to me). I realized that his goal was to keep voices from the past alive.

Mr. Jackson came up during a time when he had to be 150 percent better than everyone else. I learned that his grandparents had been born into slavery. We were both Christian and had great talks about spirituality and faith, and when my grandmother died, he helped me prepare a spiritual to sing at her funeral.

Now I view the stories he shared with me about his family as a great treasure. He was a living legacy. His life was challenging—he never had the opportunity to go to a school like ours, and this taught me to strive to be worthy of the privilege I had. As my school career progressed, I saw how important the lessons *Don't be quiet* and *Don't hide yourself* really were. As I moved forward my confidence grew. I learned more challenging music, and I made sounds I didn't think I could make! Even now, when I need to chant in church, I think of him: Be loud! Wide-open mouth!

As a preacher, and especially over the past couple of years as the church started to recognize its involvement in the slave trade and the nationwide conversation that began when George Floyd was murdered, I often find myself thinking of Mr. Jackson's stories about his grandparents and childhood. I've been able to look back on those stories and see more in them than I was able to see when I heard them in high school.

My upbringing around education feels marked by the No Child Left Behind Act. Now there's teaching to the test and there are stringent itemized expectations that don't connect to how you measure learning in a human way. Mr. Jackson was free of tests; he was free to have a different kind of relationship with his students.

Now public education is under attack. What we ask teachers to do is too much, to step into the lack of social services and support families while meeting arbitrary testing guidelines. Schools have a role in the community much like churches do. There are so few civic community institutions, and so few places where communities come to be together, to do tasks together, and even be forced to muddle through together. Schools are one of the last remaining public institutions where this is possible.

Every time I step into the pulpit, people sit still and listen to me, and I think, What a privilege this is! Our opportunities and privileges aren't guaranteed, and they should never be wasted. We luck into them and we earn them, but thanks to Mr. Jackson I understand that I must strive to be worthy of them. I thank Mr. Jackson in memorial prayers every time we have holidays. I like to think that this must make him happy.

Deborah Roberts

A dynamic college professor can
spark your passion

For many of us, college experiences have left a lasting impact on our lives. I'm one of those lucky people who found more confidence and reasons to believe I could soar thanks to encouraging professors. The first week of my freshman year at the University of Georgia, I decided that a major in theater, which I had wanted to pursue, wasn't exactly the best fit for my future. I knew that I wanted to work in television and thought acting was the best route to a TV career. But the deeply passionate theater students who often walked around campus in black leotards and pants, reciting their monologues with great purpose, just didn't seem to be my people. No offense to the drama kids who love what they do. I swallowed hard and made a frightening move: I decided to explore the UGA mass communications department. I say "frightening" because I was attending a big SEC school of twenty thousand students and the mass communications department had a national reputation. It had turned out impressive TV journalists like Charlayne Hunter-Gault and more recently, Deborah Norville, who appeared to be on the way to television stardom. I was intimidated by the sprawling new department and its sharp, top-notch professors. But I took a leap and enrolled in the Introduction to Mass Comm class, with a no-nonsense white-haired female professor. The class was huge. I grabbed a seat high up in the auditorium ready to absorb this course and the commanding teacher. Even from far away she sparked excitement. She spoke with enthusiasm about the importance of newspapers, magazines, and television and the ability of reporters to shine light on the dark corners of our society. She heralded fearless reporting and exciting careers in media, including PR, which I'd never really heard of. In an animated style, this professor, whose name I can't recall but I think was Dr. Bethune, described careers in mass comm almost as if it were a calling. I eagerly awaited each class and was disappointed that we met only three days a week. Journalism, I quickly discovered, sparked a fire in me. Television reporting was what I wanted, not television acting. I was determined to be one of those hard-charging reporters who uncovered injustices and revealed new and hopeful stories. I had found my true passion.

Soon, I found myself fully absorbed in classes like Communications Law, exploring the Pentagon Papers decision by the Supreme Court and arguing for and against legal conundrums with Professor Kent Middleton, a dashing instructor with a bit of James Bond charisma. I didn't do as well in my newspaper class with Dr. Hough, who was the quintessential college professor, complete with a tweed jacket and thinning gray hair. I knew I wasn't a print reporter, but I was inspired by his encouraging pep talks to the class. Determination and hard work, he told us, will pay off. "You'll find a job in this tough business," he told us, if we were ready to sacrifice with long hours and a tenacious spirit. I brought that spirit to my television news class, where I learned to film and report stories for a very small cable channel. Later, in my junior year, I landed a prestigious internship with Georgia public television covering the daily movements of the state legislature. I cultivated a friendship with Larry Walker, an influential lawyer and house majority leader from my hometown of Perry and learned about the wheeling and dealing of politics. It was a grueling assignment, with late nights and complex stories on the intricacies of bills and new laws that were being passed. I remember moments of exasperation and occasional tears with a fellow reporter who would become a lifelong friend, Susan Danziger, when we made mistakes in our reporting. But despite the struggles, or maybe because of them, I remembered Dr. Hough's words. I was learning grit and tenacity. I still think about him when I'm chasing a difficult story today at ABC News. Determination will pay off. College is a time of self-discovery before we step into the big world. If you're fortunate, you'll meet a professor or two who may just go that extra mile and ignite a fire in your belly. Even in a large setting, having someone who believes that you are capable and ready to take on the world can help you find your passion and your place.

Michelle Williams

Singer, songwriter, actress, author, and mental health advocate

There is a teacher who has an eye on you— go to them

Karen Portis, now retired, is a Black woman who was everyone's favorite teacher at West Middle School in Rockford, Illinois. She wasn't even an official teacher of mine; she was that teacher who would stand in the hallways saying, "Where are you going?" or "What are you doing?" Everyone in the school knew you did not cross Ms. Portis. Ms. Portis even had a way of softening a bully's heart. If Ms. Portis spent just two minutes with you, you would feel seen and heard. She'd be sure to let you know that she was here for you. A kid who might be going through hell at home, where there was chaos, knew that school was a safe place to be.

Ms. Portis went out of her way for me. She nurtured me at a time when my grades were failing, and she made sure I got in the Big Brothers and Big Sisters mentorship program.

Ms. Portis made me utilize my counselor, too. She'd say, "Do you know your grades are slipping? You are capable and smart, what is going on? I know it's not that you can't comprehend." I always felt comfortable sharing what was going on in my life with her. She was also one of the first people who saw my musical talent and encouraged me use my gift outside of the church we both attended.

I am *here* because of Ms. Portis, and I feel like she hand-picked me and said "I've got my eyes on this one." She saw me, and mind you, she had her own two boys and a husband, but she still found time for me. When we hear about violence in schools on the news, I think kids need just one teacher who can be like a mother or father, to provide a safe space.

Kids need teachers who have that look that says, *I see you*. There is at least one teacher you can go to and say, "Hey, this is a foreign feeling, I'm feeling down or I'm embarrassed to say I'm struggling in a class." Go to them!

It is so important for us to love our teachers, too. As kids we didn't know anything about putting ourselves in someone else's shoes. Kids should learn to put themselves in their teachers' shoes! They're dealing with hundreds of students every single day. Be one of the kids who make it way easier for the teacher.

Sunny Hostin

The View co-host and ABC News senior legal correspondent

Great things can happen when a teacher sees a student for who they are

When I was in third grade at St. Ann Psalms Catholic School in the South Bronx, I became a little bit mischievous because I was bored. My teachers were tired of me always answering all the questions. There was an overwhelming feeling that I should let some of the other kids answer—give others a chance! There were many times boys were called on even though they didn't know the answers. I'm doing long division at home and they're doing three times three, and you're calling on them? This frustrated me so much that I thought, Okay, fine, I won't raise my hand anymore.

With Miss Lopez things were different. She was young, with very straight, sandy-brown hair and thick glasses. She was nice, animated, and loved to teach. She had so much energy. She wasn't like other teachers, who were sometimes annoyed with me, or who always called on the boys. I sat in the front of her class and when I raised my hand, she called on me repeatedly. There were so many kids in the class, and there was a lot of noise and plenty of troublemakers and then there's me going *pick me pick me pick me!* Miss Lopez could have written my enthusiasm off as an attention thing, but she saw me and was interested. Finally, she asked, "You are always the first person to raise your hand, is it because you know all the answers?" When I responded that I did, she just said,

"Okay. We're going to figure this out." She started giving me extra workbooks while the other kids were learning what I already knew. These workbooks were color-coordinated volumes that gradually got more difficult. Three months later, she called my parents and explained that she'd been giving me standardized-test booklets that went from K to 8 and included some high-school-level work. Miss Lopez told my parents that the school I was attending wasn't going to work, and that I needed to skip a grade. My mother explained I was already ahead. My mother was a sixth-grade science teacher, and she practiced her lesson plans on me. She went to college when I was a baby. I'd sit in class with her, and as I got older, I was amazed by the learning process. My mom taught me at home, too. I was reading in kindergarten, so the school put me in first grade. By the time I got to Miss Lopez's third-grade class I was only six or seven.

My parents agreed to let me skip a grade, and that summer I went to school to learn things I'd miss in fourth grade, like the metric system. At the end of the summer, my parents were told the school probably wasn't going to work for me. They found a Catholic prep school in Manhattan, and we ultimately moved. I knew that I was different from the other students and had different abilities, but it was nice for it to be recognized. I was outgoing and had a good group of friends, but I did get a little pushback. "You're leaving the school? You're smarter than the rest of us and not going to be here? Who does that?" I felt some resentment from the other kids and probably lost some childhood friends. I felt seen, and I was happy that I wouldn't be bored anymore, but it was hard to leave the only school and neighborhood I knew.

Many of the kids were wealthy at my new school, which was on Park Avenue. The other girls lived closer. I resented the fact that I had to take two or sometimes three trains to get to school, and there were some rough kids on the train who were mean to me. I had to arrive exactly at 8:30 a.m. There was no grace period. Arriving at 8:31 a.m. was the same as arriving at 9:00 a.m. I thought this wasn't fair, so I started hanging around outside of the school like a delinquent. If a few other girls showed up late, I'd say, "You want to get breakfast?" Instead of going to homeroom late we started having breakfast at a café on Madison Avenue (the wealthy girls got the bill). It was like we started a delinquent breakfast club.

One morning, after this had been going on for months, Sister Timothy walked in to the cafe wearing her full habit. She was furious: "You're under our charge and your parents don't know where you are!" I fessed up. It had all been my idea and I didn't want other kids to get in trouble for it. She looked right at me. "You're an A student. What are you doing? You are blowing this!" I *knew* it was a terrible thing to do. I got a lot of detentions. My parents grounded me forever.

In many ways I clearly didn't belong at my new school. It was a difficult time. I felt very nerdy, and I was so much younger than everyone else. I was socially awkward. I had been raised very Catholic, and my parents were very strict. I couldn't date, or wear makeup, and I had to dress a certain way. All I was allowed to do was read books and write in my journal. I felt very different, and I looked different, being biracial. I was clearly behind in the social aspect of school, and I was on the outskirts of everything. My principal, a no-nonsense woman who was also a nun, echoed Sister Timothy's sentiments when she noticed I was coming to class late. "You have such a big future and you're ruining it. I haven't had a student as smart as you in a long time." She gave me demerits and Saturday-morning detentions, which I hated but were for my own good.

When I was in college, I realized these women saw something in me and helped me. That's what a great teacher does—sees a student for who they are: a good writer, a mathematician, a visual learner, a shy kid, a struggling student, or someone who doesn't have the confidence to let their light shine. Teachers really are changing lives and *saving* lives. I know it's hard. Teachers are so underpaid and overworked, but the profession is as important as that of doctors, lawyers, and journalists. Teachers are in the profession that saves humanity.

Some people think they are better educators than actual educators, but teaching isn't just a profession, it's an art form. This country has had a president who said that he loves the undereducated. That's because when people are undereducated you can rule them and mold them. I don't know what would have happened if Miss Lopez hadn't seen me, and I don't know what would have happened to me if Sister Timothy hadn't walked into that café. I am where I am today because of Miss Lopez and Sister Timothy.

Laysha Ward

Executive vice president &
chief external engagement officer at Target

Sometimes when you stand out,
you start to fit in

The grade-school years are all about trying to fit in. But when I was in grade school there were many things about me that made me stand out and feel self-conscious. I grew up in rural Indiana in a house with a cornfield on one side and a crop of soybeans on the other, and across the road there was lots of livestock: Chickens, hogs, and dairy cows, whose smell I can't forget. Although I went to a consolidated school with kids from neighboring towns, I was the only Black student in my class and would remain that through my senior year. I also had a speech impediment, which further set me apart from the others. As I began to find my voice and claim my space, I eventually came to realize it's okay to both fit in and stand out.

When I entered fourth grade, my teacher was Mrs. Bucher, whose last name I liked because it's pronounced "book-er," and reminded me of books and my love of reading. It was clear from the start, even to little me, that she wanted to make a difference in the lives of her students. She saw us as individuals with different strengths and challenges, and she truly listened to our needs. She pushed me to excel. And while I did well academically, I also ran my mouth a lot, which meant there was no escaping the speech impediment that hindered my ability to communicate effectively. It wasn't long before Mrs. Bucher set me up with a speech therapist, who I saw on a regular basis. Anyone who's ever had a speech impediment knows that overcoming it takes a lot of work. You basically have to relearn something you've been doing your entire life. It was hard enough being the only Black student and having trouble speaking, but being pulled out of class and having all eyes on me as I left the room made me feel even more different. But with the help of my speech therapist and the unwavering support of Mrs. Bucher and my parents, I was able to conquer my speech impediment.

Back then, I didn't fully appreciate what Mrs. Bucher had done for me—she made a conscious decision to see me and help me, ultimately changing the trajectory of my life. Neither of us had any idea that public speaking, storytelling, and connecting and co-creating with all kinds of people would become essential to my life and leadership journey—at work and in the community. Mrs. Bucher also sparked my lifelong love of learning, and taught me to seek help when I needed to get better at something. While I no longer need a speech therapist, I regularly work with a speech coach to refine my public-speaking skills. And with the help of a classmate, I recently tracked down Mrs. Bucher to thank her and share the impact she's had on my life. She was astonished and touched to hear from me after all these years. I'll never forget her or the lesson she taught me: Sometimes you have to stand out to fit in.

Debra Martin Chase

Film, television, and Broadway producer

Teachers can break down barriers

Mrs. Hauser was my sixth-grade teacher in California. She inspired me with her own story. The year before, she and her husband had taken a sabbatical and traveled around the world. They flew to Germany, bought a van, and drove all over. We spent the year studying different countries. Each student was assigned a different country, and I had Iran. Every kid made a presentation, so we all experienced our classmates' reports. We spent the year immersed in and learning about the world: We had Japanese tea ceremonies; Mrs. Hauser brought in things from Egypt to show us; we ate French cheese. She'd always wear her bangles from India. She was reliving her experience with all with us. It was a most interesting school year and the one that stands out the most for me.

My mother's sisters were great travelers. I grew up around travelers, but I could see myself as a global person because of Mrs. Hauser. She broke down the barriers and taught us that people around the world are more similar than dissimilar. When I took my first trip to Europe in college, I arrived with this perspective. I went with a friend from college, and I always say that's the summer I became a woman. It was transformative for me. We went to Spain for two months, we hitchhiked, took trains and buses. Every day was an adventure. Are we going to stay here, where next? Relying on yourself was big. As a Black woman, I felt interesting and exotic.

In the United States it's like we have to apologize to white people for being Black. I think of myself as a global citizen because of Mrs. Hauser. The seeds for that trip were sown by Mrs. Hauser. I would never have thought *you can drive around in a van*!

Education is important. In college you meet new people, live on your own, and learn how to manage your time. Those lessons are as important as what you learn in the classroom. I'm glad I had a teacher who loved sharing her life—I learned that everyone comes from their own frame of reference.

I feel incredibly fortunate to have received a great education in public schools. It was a priority with my family. Now there's not enough money, teachers are managing other duties at school as well as teaching, there's burnout. We don't value teachers in our society. We don't pay them, we don't honor them. When you don't value teachers, you don't value education or what it can do for us.

Jimmie Allen

Country artist, songwriter, and author

A teacher's influence can last a lifetime

My kindergarten teacher, Mrs. Adair, and my first-grade teacher, Mrs. Sharp, have been super supportive of me my entire life. Mrs. Adair was like Mary Poppins, rosy-cheeked and loving. We even called her Mary Poppins. Mrs. Sharp was like Dr. Quinn, Medicine Woman—she was a healer. I am in touch with them even now. They both came to my debut performance at the Grand Ole Opry. When I published my first children's book, *My Voice is a Trumpet*, I asked Mrs. Adair to read the audio edition, because I wanted the entire world to hear the same voice that read to me when I was a kid.

When I was young, I was dealing with some bad stuff. I was bipolar, but I didn't know this until I turned thirteen. I was loud, would not stop talking, and I couldn't sit still (kind of like I am now!). My teachers both figured out I was different quickly. Instead of yelling at me, telling me I was difficult, or sending me to the principal's office, both of those teachers took the time to figure out the best way to teach me so I could retain information. These teachers took their time with me and made me feel comfortable. That they thought I was capable boosted my ego *like crazy*. But confidence is a good thing; it keeps you waking up every day. It keeps you going. I teach my son that if someone tells you that you did a good job, if *you believe* you did a good job, go ahead and agree with them.

It didn't hit me how lucky I was until my mom explained to me that all teachers don't treat kids like like I was treated. Mrs. Adair didn't get married for a while. My mom once asked her about this, and she explained that she thought God was calling her to these children, and she didn't want a man or anyone else taking attention away from the kids. She just focused on being a teacher. She gave her life to everybody. I stayed connected to them both and every year I'd go back to school to see them. Now I want to pass along what they taught me to my own kids. They have given my life balance, they have fueled me when I'm feeling low, and offered peace when I have been confused. They remain two of the most valued people in my life. I'm thankful for what they've done, and my gratitude will last a lifetime.

We need to figure out a way to give teachers more money. They're tired and exhausted. But there's some kid at school they're influencing more than they could know right now. About seven years ago I tried to break it down for Mrs. Sharp: thank you. Thank you for working a job that doesn't pay enough. Thank you for working when you are overworked. Thank you for doing this even though you've been taken for granted. Thank you for making my life positive. I owe my success to the foundation I got from these two wonderful teachers.

Karen Duffy

Television personality, author, and hospital chaplain

When you're encouraged to be your authentic self, you flourish

---

There's a quote I love from Paul Bowles: "How many more times will you remember a certain afternoon of your childhood, some afternoon that's so deeply a part of your being that you can't even conceive of your life without it? Perhaps four or five times more. Perhaps not even that." His question connects me to a moment in first grade at the Holy Cross school. Miss Hennessey was my teacher. She had taught all my cousins and my brother, and I was in her class the year before she retired. My dad was a policeman, and my uncles were firefighters. Every time there was a siren, Miss Hennessey told us that we should say a prayer. This has stayed with me, and I still say a prayer every time I hear a siren. When I was a kid, I would pray for whoever was in need, but over the years I also prayed for the families. In New York City there are so many sirens, and for me it's a connection to a moment. I'm honoring the fact that someone is in need, and someone is helping them. I believe this trait is a big part of my character.

Ms. Hennessey was an older woman with white hair, but grand and elegant. She favored blue, which made her stand out in a sea of nuns dressed like penguins. She reminded me of Thurston Howell III's wife, Lovey, from *Gilligan's Island*. She was probably the same age then that I am right now, except that she was always beautifully dressed while I'm still buying my clothes in the juniors' department. I don't think she ever married. She was also like Mary Tyler Moore—she lived on her own and drove her car around town. She was more of a feminist than we would have expected. She made independence and being a grown-up seem really fascinating.

She had beautiful manners, and taught us to stand when an adult entered the room. She'd lead us through the Pledge of Allegiance in the morning, and we'd pray the rosary at lunchtime. It was a fairly strict routine. Holy Cross was a stern Catholic school, but she may have had a sense of openness during her last year there. I would often get scolded for smiling during school, because I have a rare tendon called Risorius of Santorini that pulls my face into a smirk. It's a genetic inheritance. I'd do something like grab my friend Melissa and we'd waltz around the room, since I figured I was going to get in trouble anyway. But Miss Hennessey was different. She'd laugh and say, "Okay, girls, that was funny." Hearing that from an adult was great. She was imposing, but she had a gentle side that was radiant. Miss Hennessey was the first teacher who encouraged me to be funny and happy. Girls were often told to be quiet, especially in Catholic school, and she didn't stifle that. This inspired me to speak up more. I finally saw that school wasn't a punishment; Miss Hennessey made it feel more welcoming than intimidating.

Miss Hennessey is an unsung heroine. During this tumultuous century we're living in, I find myself jumping into prayer all the time, and she launched that habit. Living in New York City, for me that means about five times a day I'm praying and sharing a bit of hope that people are going to be okay. My regularity is almost Pavlovian. I'm aware of her and I think of her every time I say a silent prayer. When I became a hospice chaplain, as part of my training we had to go to a courtroom and be a presence. My teacher said to pray for the bailiff, the judge, the family of the victim, and the accused—the entire chain. This lesson she taught me keeps expanding, and has become the backbone of my character. Miss Hennessey's influence is infinite. I've taught my son to pray when we watch the news or witness an injustice. I believe it's a mistake to do nothing because you think you can do so little; sometimes you can just carry someone in prayer.

When she was leaving school, I went to our garden with my mother to pick some of my favorite flowers for her. I presented her with a bouquet of lily of the valley, wrapped in tinfoil, but I don't think she understood the seismic influence she'd had on my life. She just had this leadership of the soul that I really admired, and I never really expressed this to her. I am GRATEFUL to Miss Hennessey for my love of reading. I am more courageous because of Miss Hennessey.

Teachers are intellectual gladiators. Teachers cultivate our inner garden. I wish teachers were rewarded the way we reward a CEO. We send kids to school before the concrete has set, their personalities still developing. Teachers have the attention of those kids and inspire them to learn life lessons. I wish the world was different and we honored them with increased pay and a holiday. We need to honor the profession more, because it takes great guts to be a teacher.

Deborah Roberts

There is wonder to be found outside
the classroom

Some of my happiest memories of middle school include lessons I learned in the classroom and outside of it. I vividly remember my spirited biology teacher, Mr. Mann. He had a broad smile and a dark brown head of hair, cut to resemble Sonny Bono's. He was a tall, lanky presence who loomed large in our classroom. When my class was studying the human skeletal system, he had a clever way of helping us understand and recall the 206 bones in the body. One day he broke into a rhythmic recitation of the leg bones. He practically waltzed through the aisles of the classroom waving his arms and legs while singing, "Femur, fibula, metatarsals, phalanges." We all laughed, but we secretly loved seeing a teacher so willing to be silly to drive home a lesson. I went home and sang the list at the dinner table, "Femur, fibula, metatarsals, phalanges." My older sister couldn't believe that a teacher would step outside the boundaries of instruction and entertain his students with a song. "Is this really a science teacher?" she asked.

Mr. Mann inspired us to have fun with tricky subject matters. And I loved his class. The day after one of our tougher exams, I remember asking him slyly, "How did I do?" He smiled and told me I passed with flying colors. I loved how proud he was to see his students do well. And I wanted to study harder and earn all As, which I did. That was a special class with a special teacher who taught me and his other students a valuable lesson—that finding the humor and fun in any subject or situation can lead to success.

Another high school instructor who left a lasting impression on me didn't exactly teach classes. She was the high school librarian, Kathy Tallon. Mrs. Tallon had a soft, comforting voice, an easy smile and round cheeks which seemed to glow when she was happy which was most of the time. She arrived at Perry High school after her husband, an Air Force pilot, was transferred to a nearby air base. They had traveled a bit and Mrs. Tallon seemed worldly and sophisticated. She also had a calm about her all the time which was amazing given the rambunctious teenagers (myself included) who often congregated in the library before and during school for various projects and to talk and laugh, something I perfected. Mrs. Tallon got to know all of us and shared details about their travels to England and beyond. And better, she asked questions about our opinions and concerns. I had never before had a teacher or librarian who cared what we thought about the world or who shared hers. But Mrs. Tallon was genuinely interested in us as people. It was clear that she wanted to inspire us to aim high and explore life. I felt a special glow anytime I stepped into the library. As time went on, I began to understand her calm spirit a bit more as she shared her interest in yoga and meditation. This small-town girl from the Deep South knew nothing of Eastern wellness practices. But my curiosity was piqued along with a couple of my friends. One day Mrs. Tallon offered to teach a yoga lesson after school in the library. I was thrilled. What a joy to delve into something new which had absolutely nothing to do with academics. Yes, I was a cheerleader and loved the physically active extracurricular part of school, but this was something completely foreign. It was exhilarating to learn how to stretch my body and to calm my mind with the different poses. I especially loved chaturanga and child's pose. The few of us who hung out to learn yoga and meditation felt grown up and sophisticated. It had never occurred to me that school could also include spiritual growth and a focus on my mental well-being. I left those sessions feeling contented and accomplished in a way that I hadn't felt when getting an A on a paper. Today i still practice yoga occasionally and meditation. And I never forget that the foundation for what we now know as "self-care" was laid in my high school library after the final bell rang.

Some of our most enduring lessons in life happened not in a classroom but after school had ended.

Keri Shahidi

Producer and actress

When a teacher believes in a student before they believe in themselves, they blossom

---

I come from a family of teachers. My grandfather was a principal, my grandmother taught and tutored into her nineties, and my dad has a PhD in education. My family was living in Madison, Wisconsin, and rather than take me to the local school my father chose to drive me to the Longfellow Elementary School, which was Spanish speaking. He wanted to surround me with brown, Black, and immigrant kids and teachers. My teacher was Miss Gerry Parish. She was in her mid-twenties and looked as young as a cousin of mine. She was the first female Black teacher I had. To this day she's the reason why I tell my kids to look in the dictionary if they don't know the meaning of a word.

We knew I was academically advanced, and by the end of fourth grade it was clear I was really good at math. "Did you finish all that already? Let's get you something else." Miss Parish often gave me math packets, and as a girl who grew up with the mantra *She who can, does*, I finished them. But when she gave me a math packet for the summer, I panicked. I asked my parents to let me transfer to the school my brother went to, and this was the worst decision of my life. The new school was the opposite of Longfellow Elementary. I was sad about what I had left behind. Gone were the open classrooms and attention to different learning styles. I was one of two Black kids. One day a teacher put me out in the hallway for talking (for the record, I *wasn't* talking). She forgot about me for the entire afternoon. When she opened the door at the end of the day to let the kids out, she was surprised to see me there. I had gone from being seen by Miss Parish to being invisible.

As I progressed to the sixth grade, I took a piece of Miss Parish with me. I took my confidence along to the new school. I took a knowingness that I was smart and that has *never* gone away. Looking back at women in STEM, I really think it's seeded by having a teacher who believes in you before you believe in yourself. Miss Parish was so confident in her ability to teach. In her classroom I felt like I was getting one-on-one attention, even though there were many of us. She managed to give everyone focused attention. I felt supported as a young Black woman, and when I walked out of her classroom I was walking out ahead of the game.

Miss Parish is foundational to why I am so confident as a Black woman. She hit all the intersections: She was smart, kind, confident, athletic, and she even looked like me. She *already was* everything that I wanted to be. The importance of having a Black female teacher trickled down to my kids, and I'm glad my son is having that same opportunity. I've always carried Miss Parish's spirit with me. When I worked in Spanish education, I made sure to bring along her excitement. I am blossoming because of Miss Parish, and I'm still blossoming. I'm still discovering what I'm capable of, and it feels like there is no limit to what I can do.

I feel honestly terrible about the situation that many teachers find themselves in, but I want to be supportive. The opportunity is there. I'll ask my kids' teachers, *How can we support you?* I'm still in touch with Miss Parish. I've had the opportunity to let her know how she impacted me. It turns out that she had something to tell me, too. "You know that math packet back at the end of fourth grade was just for fun, right? I wasn't going to grade it!"

Lorraine Toussaint

Trinidadian American actress

A good teacher is the tonic to something toxic

When I was nine years old, I lived in the Caribbean, where the educational system was very different. Children were seen and not heard. It was very punitive, and this was considered okay at the time. I went to the San Fernando Government School, which had strict rules and uniforms. The educational system was designed to crush a child's spirit. When a child's spirit was broken, they were malleable, manageable, and controllable. This system almost broke me. I was an artsy child who was a daydreamer and an unconventional learner. I actually had to sit in the corner facing the wall while wearing a tiny cap that said "dunce." My report cards said I talked too much and daydreamed too much (this turned out to be the good news, because now that's what I get paid for). My teacher told me I was unteachable. I was failing, and the more I failed the more I was punished. The more I was punished the more I failed. I was withering away.

Then I was transferred to Mrs. K's classroom. She was a light-skinned, young Black woman who was thick and strong. She had thick kinky hair that she wore in long plaits. She had full lips and a big gap between her teeth just like me. She was bowlegged and had the hairiest legs you've ever seen on a human being. When I was looking at Mrs. K, I was seeing myself, and it was a beautiful thing. She was the first teacher who ever saw me. It's like I fell in love with her because she was so kind. I thought she was the most beautiful woman in the world after my mother, and when I got older, I let my legs get hairy to be more like her. She talked to her students like they were tiny human beings that deserved respect and kindness, and had their own voice. She honored the humanity in little kids. I began to come alive academically in her class, but more than anything else I felt safe for the first time in school.

I am forever grateful to Mrs. K, because she literally saved my life. Thanks to her I was no longer an invisible, unteachable, throwaway child. She helped me to believe that I was a beautiful girl. As a child I was like a small animal trying to earn the right to be recognized as a human being, and she did that for me. She was incredibly patient, and not interested in authority and power or rendering children powerless. She empowered them by seeing them and letting them *know* they are seen.

I can't believe the way we undervalue teachers, not in just this country but in most of them. Teachers are often with our kids for more waking hours than their parents are. Teachers have the ultimate power to shape, guide, direct, and nurture children. Children are sponges and they are vulnerable. Teachers can be toxic, like my first teacher, or a tonic, like Mrs. K. It's a holy calling to be a teacher. A holy, righteous calling. The ones that perceive it as such are the ones who are infinitely impactful to our children. If I could share my gratitude with Mrs. K, I would say: *Thank you so much, you have no idea how you've influenced all aspects of my life. You taught me that I have value. I saw my worth in your eyes. You gave me the courage to go against the grain and do things no one else in my family had done. You sparked me in a way that no one else had. I am ALIVE because of you. I see myself and value myself because of you. I celebrate my Afrocentricity because there was a full-lipped, bowlegged, hairy-legged woman with a gap between her teeth during a crucial time in my life. Because of you I understand how much power teachers have, and now my daughter wants to be a teacher.*

Brit Bennett

Bestselling author

A little encouragement can lead to great things

Mrs. McGann, my third-grade teacher at the Ivy Ranch Elementary School, was a white teacher, but she was the first teacher who taught me about Black history. It was an important experience, having a teacher who was interested in Black culture and Black history. None of my teachers had ever taught this, and no one had ever assigned Black books. Mrs. McGann taught us about the Harlem Renaissance, and this was the first time I had encountered that. It made an impression on me and my parents because they were used to being my only source of information about Blackness since they knew I wasn't getting it in school. Mrs. McGann was intentional about teaching Black history and Black literature. While there were a handful of Black kids in the class, most of the kids were white. This struck me and my family, because it was such an unusual experience to learn about Black culture at the time. It left an impression on me as far as what I was interested in reading and writing. This was a pivotal year—I was starting to shift towards middle school, and I was starting to think about myself differently.

Third grade was also the first time I read a novel. Mrs. McGann noticed that I was reading beyond the class reading list, and she *gave* me a copy of *The Outsiders* by S. E. Hinton. She wasn't letting me borrow it, I got to *keep* it, and that was so exciting. "I think you'll like this," she said. The book was about young people and teenagers, and it moved me. The author was very young when she wrote the book, and it hadn't occurred to me that you don't have to be fifty years old to write a novel. This book took the lives of young people seriously, and I felt like Mrs. McGann took me seriously even though I was eight years old. She went beyond the scope of her responsibilities by giving me this book and it lit a fire in me. It was so cool, this person seeing something in me and offering this book to me. It set me on my path. Reading *The Outsiders* made me want to be a novelist.

We had a pet snake in our classroom, and kids got to take it home for the weekend. I desperately wanted to take it home, but my parents were like, *absolutely not*. Mrs. McGann came over to our house and gave me a toy stuffed snake because she knew how disappointed I was. Now that I'm an adult and have friends who are teachers, I know how hard their jobs are and how much it takes to go above and beyond. Mrs. McGann had her own family and a million other students, but she still made me feel seen, and this really struck me.

When I became a writer, people constantly asked, "How did you know this is what you want to do?" I looked back at the origin of this, and I realized I started writing around this time. I wanted to write fiction in third and fourth grade. I would write and type up stories on the family computer. The moment I became more of a reader, I could also pivot to seeing myself as a writer.

I was lucky to have teachers who encouraged me along the way. My eleventh-grade English teacher, Mrs. Esteban, was one of the most passionate teachers I've ever met. This was at a point when I was finished with high school, and ready to move on to college. Mrs. Esteban wanted us to be purposeful about how we engaged with language. She also defended us and vouched for our potential. Once she got upset when we were grading each other's papers in class. A couple of girls were mocking a paper that was badly written, and Mrs. McGann wasn't having it: "There are people who school comes easily to, and there are others that have to work very hard." School came easily to me, but this was an important reminder to be humble and kind. I had the opportunity to meet Mrs. Esteban for lunch a few years ago, and it was cool to see her as an actual adult. She asked me if I wanted a drink, and I thought, This is so weird!

I went to Stanford for college. I was in class with kids who went to private schools and boarding schools, and I was intimidated sometimes, but I knew I had a good education. I don't take my educational experiences for granted. I had teachers who went above and beyond. My gratitude was renewed when I saw what my teacher friends were going through during the pandemic. The difficulties they had interacting with parents and bosses, things that go beyond what actually happens in the classroom. In college a teacher told me to apply to grad school, and I was fortunate to have educators saying yes to me, and encouraging me along the path I was following. It wasn't that I was a great writer when I was eight years old, but so many people get one nasty comment, and they never write again. No teacher ever said to me *I don't think you're talented* or *You should stop writing*. Kids are so impressionable, and if a teacher isn't encouraging a kid can abandon an interest. If a teacher had told me at eight years old that I wasn't a good writer, I probably would have stopped writing.

I am a better writer because of Mrs. McCann and Mrs. Esteban. Mrs. McCann inspired me to become a novelist and storyteller. We read nonfiction in Mrs. Esteban's class, and she taught me to write well-reasoned opinion pieces, which I had never done before. The first piece of writing I ever published was an opinion piece. These teachers set me on track and nudged me in these directions. Sometimes, when writing is difficult, I think back to that eight-year-old girl who was writing a story about coyotes. She was excited to read anything, less self-conscious, and totally free. To meet teachers at a time when you are so vulnerable and free is really important— it's so empowering.

Agenia Walker Clark, EdD

Corporate board director and nonprofit CEO

The most magical words are "You are smart"

Every morning in Toulminville, Alabama, you could look out your window and see a trail of Black children making their way down the road to the Stanton Road Elementary School. Schools might have been desegregated, but in 1966 my community and my school were still predominantly Black. While I didn't think of myself as a standout student in second grade, there was one thing I knew for sure—I was a Chatty Cathy. I talked *all* the time. I never stopped. So, when I looked up to find Ms. Sarah Green Walker standing in front of my desk looking down at me, I was terrified. I had never gotten in trouble at school before, and this teacher looked stern. Ms. Walker said, "I'm moving you. Get up and bring your desk and chair with you."

This prompted a chorus of *ooooohs* peppered with an occasional *She is in TROUBLE!* I was expecting to be stashed in a corner where there would be no one for me to talk to, so I was surprised when Ms. Walker pointed to the front of the room. She leaned in closely to me and spoke in a gentle voice, "I'm making you sit next to me because you are the smartest child in this room. That's why you talk all the time, because you're smart and you have things to say. I'm not punishing you, but you are going to be my helper. And to be clear, you're not going to disrupt the class anymore, right? Most of these kids aren't as smart as you."

Not only was this the first time I was told I was smart, but it was the first time I thought about what being smart *really meant*. Ms. Walker had planted the seed that maybe being smart was about something bigger than handing in a perfect math worksheet or acing a spelling test. I started to become curious about where "being smart" could take me. I walked out of school later that day feeling there was something *to me*. I always thought Ms. Walker looked like a queen, and her demeanor demanded respect. That this educated, elegant woman who always looked immaculate and fresh in her dresses with stockings and matching pumps (not easy to pull off in the Alabama heat) saw something *in me* that made me want to take school more seriously.

She wasn't kidding about helping her, either. "Agenia, I'm going to work with these children. A few kids are still struggling with yesterday's lesson, and I need you to help them." I never knew I had the capacity to help anyone learn anything. That this queen thought I was worthy enough to be helpful to another student blew my mind. Two weeks later I was allowed to move my desk back to its original position, but I was no longer interested in talking. I wanted to learn as much as I could, and over time the classroom and the learning process became my comfort zone.

When I entered middle school, everything was still segregated, and that deep-South culture persisted. In seventh grade I had an opportunity to take an entrance exam through my church, and if I passed, I would be able to attend St. Paul's Episcopal College Preparatory School. I passed the test and I got in. Everything at the preparatory school was different. There were no other Black students, and for the first time I had white teachers. The standards at this school were high, and much was demanded from us. St. Paul's gave me some of the best education I've had, and there was nothing thrown at me that I couldn't handle. Looking back to that pivotal moment in second grade, I could see that Ms. Walker wanted me to know something early on—that if I focused and paid attention there would be opportunities for me to grab on to, and I needed to be ready for those opportunities. I excelled at St. Paul's, then went on to college, and eventually pursued a master's degree and a PhD. There's a good chance this would not have happened if Ms. Walker hadn't whispered to a chatty little Black girl . . . *You are smart.*

My working-class parents were grateful for the guidance Ms. Walker gave me, and my father, who was an excellent baker, made her one of his specialties—German chocolate cake. I remember how appreciative Ms. Walker was when she received that cake, but I still regret that I didn't go back to see her again at St. Paul's. I would have told her that there have been many other "chairs" in my life—in the form of goals I'm trying to reach, career wins, or big life changes. When facing challenges that seem insurmountable, I can still feel myself sitting in that chair next to her desk, and I draw strength from those life-altering words I heard so many years ago: *You are smart.* I believe Ms. Walker knew in her heart that she might not see the outcome of her gift, she just gave freely. And that's why with each success and with each crucial moment of my life I take a moment to reflect on how I got into the very chair I'm sitting in. I tell myself, *Okay, you got here! But are you giving everything you have to give?* That's the best way I know to repay Ms. Walker, to do my best with every opportunity, occasionally stopping along the way to connect with another little girl who needs to hear those three magical words. *You are smart.*

Francesca Serritella

Bestselling author and columnist

Teachers are a mirror of your best self

My seventh-grade ELA teacher in my school outside of Philadelphia was Mrs. LoGiudice. She was a tiny, brunette Italian woman who looked like a petite Marisa Tomei. She was warm and enthusiastic but held high expectations for her students. She was the teacher I saw first thing every morning. I had always liked school, but I was a little nervous that year because I was new to the area. Seventh grade is also a time when you're trying to figure out who the grown-up version of yourself is. I was trying to discover my identity.

Mrs. LoGiudice was a vibrant woman who ignited my love of reading. She ran the Edgar Allan Poe Club, and I wanted to join after we had read one of his stories and I liked it. I showed up at the assigned time to discover it was just me and her. I felt a little embarrassed, like I'd chosen something uncool. It turned out to be a blessing in disguise, because we got to geek out about Edgar Allan Poe together. She also introduced me to Charles Dickens. She had me read *A Tale of Two Cities*. It was my first grown-up, classic book and I felt so accomplished when I finished it. It has this great romance plot, but also a villain, Madame Defarge, who was my favorite, and she turned out to be Mrs. LoGiudice's favorite, too. To look at a book from a different angle and have my opinion validated was great.

She did a lot of creative-writing prompts in class, and I loved them. My mom, the writer Lisa Scottoline, was still building her career at that time, and it was inspiring to watch, but it really felt like her own thing. Mrs. LoGiudice was the first person who helped me see *myself* as a writer. I didn't want to write to be just like my mother; Mrs. LoGiudice taught me that it's possible to find your own path and your own tastes. I learned that I could have my own journey. Recently my mom reminded me that when I published my first book, Mrs. LoGiudice sent me a copy of a letter I had given her at the end of seventh grade. In the letter I thank her for an amazing year, and I talk about Dickens and Madame Defarge. But the part of the letter I'd forgotten writing was this:

Who knows? Maybe one day you'll see my name on the cover of a book everyone is talking about. They'll ask, When did you know you wanted to be an author? And I'll say, 'About seventh grade.'

That confidence kind of takes me by surprise. I wasn't that confident a kid going into seventh grade, and that girl wouldn't have written something so bold or seen herself that way. There was a self-determination evident that I didn't have before. Mrs. LoGiudice helped me embrace my nerdiness and quirkiness. We embraced the fun and the joy of reading and writing. As an adult I also realized that my reading and writing taste has a bit of a dark streak: gothic literature, psychological suspense, surreal horror. Mrs. LoGiudice was the first warm sunny person I met who also shared those tastes.

Her class felt like the biggest hug, and I'm grateful to her for that. That year involved a lot of change for me: My parents were divorced, and my families were reblending on both sides. It was the year Columbine happened, and it was unfathomable that such violence could take place in the classroom. Mrs. LoGiudice's classroom felt like a refuge, a stable place that felt like a second family. It was great to feel accepted and validated.

I have sympathy for teachers because they are the hub of education and the community. They are the connective tissue in a neighborhood or district, and we are asking more of them than ever. If they have to be a cop and a therapist, and we keep adding new roles for them, we are not freeing them to do what they do best. Teachers need more support across the board.

I am joyful because of Mrs. LoGiudice. She brought so much joy and enthusiasm to reading and writing and taught me it could be fun. Whenever someone talks about teachers they love I think of her, and it puts a smile right on my face. Teachers deserve so much credit. They provide launch pads and serve as mirrors to our best selves. What they do is sacred.

Sergio Hudson

Fashion designer

Everything can be done better

I was a fat and insecure kid who wanted to be a designer. I was picked on and called terrible names because I was gay. I was an overachiever, and I let my talent mask my insecurities. I went to Bauder College, and that's where I met Cassandra Harrison. Ms. Harrison was a beautiful, slender, Black woman who had long dreadlocks and wore Afrocentric clothing—I couldn't believe it! She was a regal figure who commanded respect, and had creativity oozing from her pores. She had *done the work* before she decided to start teaching. Ms. Harrison was a pattern maker; she worked with Bob Mackie and owned her own clothing store for years.

At first design school made me miserable (especially the math). You don't get to make designs until your second or third year of school. I wasn't showing up for classes and I was getting Fs. At one point I almost got kicked out, but the school gave me another chance. That's when Ms. Harrison set me straight. "I'm disappointed in you. You're messing this up. You have something these kids don't have, but you can't rest on that. You need a good work ethic. You need to think like a perfectionist. If you want to do this, you need to change something." This was a wake-up call for me, because I hated the idea of letting Ms. Harrison down. I went from getting Fs in my classes to making As. I would spend time in her workroom, where I learned what it really meant to be a perfectionist. She taught me *everything can be done better*. This lesson was powerful, and it guided me when I started making clothes for people with my own two hands. I realized, Wow, I would have let that slide if it wasn't for Mrs. Harrison. "Okay" is never enough, and I think this comes through in my work. I look at samples from production and think, That zipper can be better. This is why retailers are always happily surprised by the high quality of my garments.

As I got closer to graduation, I realized what a gift Ms. Harrison had given me. By that time, we had grown so close that I called her Mom. I remember she said to me, "My work here is done." We keep in contact on Facebook. I've told her that I appreciate her for changing my life. I was on a collision course with failure, and it was her influence that kept me on track. She was proud after my big moment: dressing Michelle Obama for Joe Biden's inauguration. She wanted to put great designers of color into the world, and I was able to do that for her. I think teachers are the gateway to people's future. Teachers are underestimated and overlooked—they are as crucial as doctors or lawyers, and should be trained and paid accordingly. We couldn't go on without teachers; they are as important as the air we breathe. This is an important job, and not everyone can or should do it. Ms. Harrison excelled at teaching in every way, and I owe her a lot.

Anna Deavere Smith

Actress, playwright, and professor

Being seen can open a student's mind

My junior high school experience was terrible. Western High School in Baltimore was the oldest public girls' school in the country, and it was one of the first to integrate. For a Black girl this wasn't a good environment. I was nervous about high school; I didn't know what to expect. On the very first day, I'm walking down the hall when I see a short, elegant Black woman. "You're a Smith!" This dignified woman, Mrs. Essie Smith (no relation), knew who I was because she had taught all my aunts and uncles. It felt so good to be seen and recognized in a place where I expected to be obscure. High school would be the place where I started to come out of my shell.

Mrs. Essie Smith became a very important person in my life. I would come to her office and hear stories about her travels. French was my favorite class; I was crazy about it. She was fluent in French and told me about her trips to Paris and Nice. I heard stories about French women not wearing bras! She opened my eyes to a bigger world and lit a fire under my desire to live bigger. I wanted a cosmopolitan, international kind of life like hers. She stimulated my mind.

Many years later I went back to Baltimore to perform one of my plays. My mother and Mrs. Essie Smith were both there. They came to see me backstage in my tiny dressing room. Mrs. Essie Smith was still elegant, but she was in her nineties by then, and her hat was askew. As soon as my mother was out of earshot she said, "I can see it now, your mother and I would sit in my office and say, 'We've got to get her out of here!'" While I've taken full credit for my life, it was interesting to find out she and my mother had been conspiring to get me out into the world all that time. I am a woman of the world because of Mrs. Essie Smith.

Kitt Shapiro

Business owner and author

Little pearls of wisdom can make a big impact

Whenhen I think of people who have taught me things, the first person I think of is my mother, Eartha Kitt. I know we can all say that about our parents, but there was a teacher who influenced my mother that she never forgot. When my mother was living in the South, in a terrible, abusive situation, a teacher put a hand on her shoulder and said, "You have the hand of God on your shoulder." My mother talked about this until the day she died. My mother believed that all of us were teachers, even if it's only for a moment.

There's a photograph of the two of us looking out the window. My mom is pointing to something, and it reminds me that everything she did was a teaching moment. Once, when I was a little girl, we were in the vegetable garden and there was a slug crawling on the ground. I thought it was disgusting. "You've got to kill it!" Mom looked at me and said, "You don't have a right to kill it just because you don't like the way it looks. It doesn't mean it doesn't have the right to be here." They seemed like throwaway words, but these little pearls of wisdom were so meaningful. My mom really understood the impact parents have.

I went to a French school in California from the moment I started school until I went to college. My mom sent me to this school because she wanted me to be bilingual and to learn about the world beyond the United States.

I adored Mrs. Coleman, the art teacher. She was a wavy-haired eccentric and was the only one in the entire school who didn't speak French. We all felt safe expressing ourselves artistically in that class, because she believed art was about expression; talent was irrelevant. But Madame Kabbaz, who oversaw the school, had the biggest impact on me. She was French Moroccan, exotic-looking, elegant, and always dressed to the nines (which isn't the norm in laid-back California).

I attended school over the summer one year, and I was surprised when my teacher asked me to stand in the hallway. I had no idea what was going on and I thought I was in trouble (turns out it was because the other students were being unruly). I was crying, standing there like an outcast, worried about what I had done. Here comes Madame Kabbaz, the highest-ranking person in the school. She was headed my way, and I felt more panicked. She didn't scold me. She simply asked me what happened, and then suddenly we were going across the street to her house, where I was given a Twinkie. *I was thrilled*. This was a huge treat, because my mother would never allow me to eat such a thing. It was such a relief to be reassured and receive kindness from this wonderfully elegant woman. I felt safe in her presence, and I could relax.

Madame Kabbaz had a big personality. She was very strict but was also gregarious. There was something about her that made me want to do better. I think as humans we want to rise to the occasion, and some people have a way of creating this desire. She looked formal but didn't *feel* formal. She put people at ease with the funny stories she would tell in her heavy French accent. It was always fun to listen to her.

Teaching is *the most* important job. Teachers are the true heroes, even though they aren't the ones who are getting the financial and emotional support that they deserve. Teachers are incredibly under-rated. We all know that teachers are not as respected as they should be. Teachers are encountering children every day who are filled with all sorts of emotions. It's not just about academics anymore—some kids eat their only meals at school! It is so important for everyone to have access to education across the board. It should be as even and as fair as it can be. We've managed to show appreciation for healthcare workers (at least somewhat). Teachers are in the most difficult situations day in and day out, dealing with a multitude of different personalities. Teachers are so deserving of honor.

Abby Huntsman

Television host and political commentator

School should be a safe space
to express yourself

My upbringing was like that of a military brat. We moved basically every year of my life and I went to four different high schools. When I think about teachers, it's a little bit different for me. I wasn't someone who would ever be under a teacher's wing for very long, so when a teacher made an impact on me, it goes to show that it was a big one.

A teacher who changed the trajectory of my life was my English teacher my senior year of high school, Susan Lake. The reason I loved her was because she was able to do for us kids in high school what is so special for teachers: She challenged us, but also helped us find our passion. And helped us find the confidence in ourselves to find that passion. She was a perfect balance of brutal honesty and toughness, so she made you want to keep trying, but there was enough warmth for you to be able to openly express yourself in the class. She encouraged us to think bigger. At the end of our year, we all had to read our final paper in front of the class. Some kids wrote very personal essays about themselves. I'll never forget because much of my upbringing took place in Utah and it's a much more conservative environment. There was a boy in the class who opened up about being gay in that paper. He read it in front of our entire class. I think that was the biggest sign about Ms. Lake, the way she allowed people to feel that comfort in her presence, but also challenged them to think about their feelings and to put them to words. She was someone I stayed in touch with. We weren't just her students, she wanted to help us grow and blossom and find a beautiful life and a passion. For her it wasn't just teaching, it was, How do I save these kids?

That year my dad was running for governor of Utah, and it was a little uncomfortable for me in school. I just wanted to be normal, and I remember feeling really safe in Ms. Lake's class and feeling like I could let my mind wander and do what I wanted to do. I gave her a lot of credit for that. When I say she was tough, I mean there were some moments where she wasn't always the nicest, but I think that's because she expected a lot from us.

I was always a really motivated, outgoing person because I was forced to reintroduce myself constantly. I was always the new girl. I was also one of seven kids, so I was looking for a little bit of individualism. That period of my life I just wanted to focus on the things that really got me up in the morning. I loved theater and grew up doing musical theater. I loved writing and poetry.

Ms. Lake was able to really zone in on me as an individual when I think I really needed it. She told me about real-life things, like her husband left her because he was gay. She wasn't just a teacher, but also someone I built a relationship with.

She was a bruiser in all ways. I think her toughness on me was to show me she was going to make me put in the work, and this made me feel very normal. I had been changing schools all the time, and she also gave me the confidence to know that I could *belong*. This sense of belonging was really important to me, and it made those years much better. She also encouraged my passion—I love writing and being creative and she urged me down that road.

The other person who stuck out to me was someone I knew during my first year of college. It was Governor Ed Rendell from Pennsylvania, of all people. He taught a class at Penn on Monday nights to us young kids, letting them in on his world, what he did every day. He didn't have to do that, he was one of the busiest people. He was governor at the time, and involved in everything, but he never missed a class. He was there before we got there, he stayed until after we left. He loved teaching the students about politics and communications. He did not act like he was governor; he just came to class because he really cared about teaching, and he wanted to help the next generation give back and be involved. I love it when people can put the ego aside and ask, How can I encourage people to believe in themselves? To have someone from that world teach a class was pretty special. I was not afraid to fail because both of those teachers put me in positions where I felt secure. They had patience with me, but they also pushed me enough to find the confidence needed to thrive in the world. I know that there will be moments in my children's lives growing up where I won't be able to give them confidence in a certain area, and I hope they will have the experience of connecting with a life-changing teacher like I did.

Dawn Porter

Award-winning documentary filmmaker

There's no need to separate being creative from being smart

I was the kind of kid who looked forward to the start of a new school year. The new outfits and the fresh, sharp pencils that signified the beginning of the year were exciting to me. Mrs. Murner, who was both my third-grade and fifth-grade teacher, made a huge impression on me. There were books in her classroom everywhere, and cozy rugs and dioramas were always on display. She didn't just have us do spelling and math, she let us know that art and imagination were important, too.

Every day we had a story hour. It was always a peaceful time. The entire class would be lying on the floor on a cozy carpet while she read to us from her desk. Listening to someone read is important; it can be so calming. Mrs. Murner had each student bring in their favorite book for her to read from. When it was my turn, I brought in *The Last of the Really Great Whangdoodles* by Julie Andrews Edwards (it would be a long time before I realized the book was written by *the* Julie Andrews). It was a story about a magical land that can only be reached through the imagination. The last Whangdoodle lives there, and a group of children go into this magical land to try to find it. They battle all sorts of interesting creatures along the way. I loved all the details about the flowers, the topography, and how tastes and colors were different there. As my teacher read my book to us, I thought about how it's possible to create everything in a world to be exactly how you wanted it. This wasn't just a story to her, she also managed to turn it into a lesson that encouraged all of us to build our own worlds. She thought being creative was being smart. She didn't separate the two, and that made it exciting to be in her class. Mrs. Murner was the opposite of the *get your head out of the clouds* teacher.

This was the 1970s, and it was a difficult time. There was racial strife, gas shortages with long lines at the pump, and conflicts around busing. People's parents were getting laid off and some were divorcing. Black kids who didn't want to be there were being bused far away from home, and our small school suddenly felt very tense. But walking into Mrs. Murner's classroom was like walking into Narnia. Her classroom felt safe, like an oasis of possibility where everyone was full of potential. It wasn't that I forgot about what was going on outside, but while I was in her classroom it wasn't the primary thing to worry about. I didn't realize it then, but it was important to have the positive sense of self I got from being around her. When I did have to confront racial issues, I knew who I was.

Mrs. Murner was the first teacher who made me feel smart. She put me in accelerated groups for English and math. She didn't say anything about it, she just put me there. She also managed to do this in a way that didn't make other kids feel behind. She encouraged imagination and wanted us to write our own stories. She taught me to see bigger: *You can* write books—you can do more than what you just see around you! I believe it was Mrs. Murner who planted the seed of a filmmaker in me, and because of her I learned that *I can* make up my own worlds.

Rachael Ray

Celebrity chef, entrepreneur, and author

We are all teachers sometimes

I'm lucky in that I've had a lot of people in my life who have influenced me. I grew up in a small town in a very conservative Upstate New York community where I went to public school. I had a lot of great teachers, and I've also had great mentors over the years. These people have made me who I am, but it was my mother and grandfather who set me on the right path.

My grandfather Emmanueli, who was one of fourteen children, came over from Italy when he was a kid, and he lived with us when I was a little girl. My mother was working long hours in restaurants, and he took care of me around the clock. We always played games or cooked together. If he was sitting, I'd be on his lap (even if he was in the middle of a card game with his friends. I was probably the only kid around who smelled like an old man). He used to teach me about the cycle of life, when I would ask him curious questions like, "Why do fish die?" He really prepared me for school, because when I was in kindergarten, he taught me how to read. He always taught me to value friendship and appreciate sports. He'd make me laugh by reenacting sporting events for me. He knew how to grow vegetables and raise rabbits for protein (when my mom was a girl, she learned to stop naming the rabbits). He was generous, too—at Christmas he'd buy treats and new pairs of shoes for all the local kids.

On one of my first days of school I'm dressed like I'm going to church. I was in a cute dress (no jeans for me), and the other kids were laughing at me. I had a book with me, and the teacher took it away because she thought it was arrogant of me to bring it when the other children didn't know how to read yet. Lunch was even more awkward. My grandpa made my lunch and he had packed me one of my favorites, a sardine sandwich. The other kids couldn't believe what I was eating. I came home in hysterical tears that day. Grandpa put me on my bed and dabbed my swollen eyes with a cold washcloth. He told me to just breathe, and he got me calmed down. He tapped my head and said, "What's in here?" I had no idea what he was talking about. "It's your brain. You are very smart, and you know how to read—that's a wonderful thing." I grew calmer and he added, "What do you have to complain about? You have ten fingers and toes, you've got your brain! In life we must choose whether we want to laugh or cry! There will always be another day." If it wasn't for Grandpa's calm and comforting words, I don't know how I would have ever set foot in that classroom again.

My mother, who is now eighty-eight years old, worked hundred-hour weeks most of her life. I have never seen anyone work harder. My mother is an absolute beast even though she's not even five feet tall. You have to be tough to work in restaurants. She also never asked anyone to do a job she wasn't willing to do herself. For many years, my mom was our breadwinner. She worked tirelessly and never complained about it.

She would scrimp and save to take us on little adventures. Maybe a Broadway show in New York City. She wanted to give us exposure to the world and to the idea that it was bigger than where we came from. She showed us that there were other places to feel joyful about and were much larger than the community that we grew up in.

Both my mother and grandfather taught me about the power of hard work, and it is the primary principle of everything that I do. I was taught that work is a gift, and it all begins with the respect for work itself. Work is a privilege, and my mother made sure that I understood this, and if you don't treat work with respect, it can be taken away from you. My grandfather and mother put me in a position to be ready to learn and work hard at school. For me, work is the foundation for everything, whether it's school, building a company, writing a book, or creating a show. The principles they shared with me are the building blocks of my entire life.

Kim Powers

Author and writer for ABC's 20/20

A tough teacher can give you the
DNA of your career

When I think about teachers who have impacted my life, my mind goes back to one teacher instantaneously. This was a teacher I didn't like very much, not because she was mean, but because she was so tough. She made me work harder than I probably have ever worked in my life, and this was at a completely formative time. I was in the seventh grade, and my English teacher was named Mrs. Huey. We all disliked her so much that we called her Mrs. Shooey. Only a clever seventh grader could come up with a name like that! This was the advanced English class, and we probably did things at a higher level than a lot of her other classes did.

Whenever I think of her, I remember a stout woman with gray hair. She was always well dressed in a suit or a dress, never pants. Her face was powdered, and she always wore lipstick. I picture her at the blackboard, where she was constantly diagramming sentences. She was such a taskmaster about the real nuts and bolts of the English language. We did everything from studying short stories and poems to diagramming sentences. I was a great reader. I had started reading when I was four or five years old, but diagramming sentences seemed impossible at the time. It was the first time I was hearing words like "adjectives" and "adverbs." It was such a revelation to me, and I worked so hard. Us students would go home after school and get on the phone and help each other. I always talked to my rival in English, Pat Murray, and we'd go over what we did. I didn't especially enjoy this, because I wanted to just coast along and discuss ideas, but diagramming sentences was one of the building blocks of what I do. Mrs. Huey required a lot, and the homework was tough. We'd read books and stories that seemed massive and hard to read, and wrote analytical papers. The sign of a good teacher is that they push you beyond what you think you can do. My living is about writing now, both at ABC and the books I write. Mrs. Huey gave me the DNA of my writing career.

In high school I had another impactful English teacher, Myra Frances. She had us write two pages in a journal every week, and it seemed insurmountable, even though we could write about anything we wanted to. Right before summer, my church choir had gone to Puerto Rico to perform all over the island. This was the beginning of my starting a sustained narrative as I wrote about that summer in Puerto Rico. We were playing hand bells, and I was so bad at music I was only allowed to do the heavy bells, because they were only played once or twice in a song. We carried these heavy bells all over Puerto Rico. I even started playing around with a novel that summer; I called it *Handbells for Jesus*.

I started to write other things. We read *Julius Caesar*, and I wrote an essay. When Ms. Frances gave it back to me, she said, "My son is in college, and I had him read your essay. He thinks your writing is better than anyone in his class." This was so encouraging! Sometimes I'd add little inside jokes for her in my papers. She always responded to them, and that was encouraging, too. She helped me select stories for my oral-interpretation readings for competitions and gave me extra reading when I had finished something. She was shaping my education and my life as a reader.

I was very active in drama and was in the lead in many plays. I usually played a sensitive young man, or the complete opposite, an old man. When I went off to college, my plan was to go back and be a high school theater teacher. I loved drama in high school, and I loved my teachers. I took education classes, but by my sophomore year I was leaning toward being an actor or a director. That I wanted to be a high school teacher tells me that my teachers had done something special. I saw teaching as a very worthwhile career.

My mother taught fourth grade, and my aunt and two of my cousins were also teachers. It just kills me to remember how worn-out my mother was. At the end of the day, she was so tired (and class sizes were likely smaller then) that it felt like she didn't have much left to give to her own children. My mom also used her own money for basic supplies like glue, construction paper, and scissors. I see the prohibitions on teachers: what you can't say, books being taken out of libraries because some parents object, the "Don't Say Gay" bill, or the fact that in some places teachers can't call a trans student by their new name and have to use their birth name. I see the anecdotal reports of teachers quitting. I'm sad for teachers and students. Teachers are so terrified to have something encouraging be interpreted as negative. My teachers went the extra mile with openness, and it was applauded. Because of what my teachers taught me about reading I learned about the world and how to navigate life with all its ups and downs. Mrs. Huey and Myra Frances were like bookends. First, I was taught the basics, then I had the freedom to let my mind wander and follow it wherever it took me. In the end, it all took me toward a career in writing.

James Farmer

Southern author, interior designer, and speaker

Teachers can make great literature come alive

My mother and grandmother were teachers. Aside from their instruction in life, they also instilled in me a love for writing and reading. Their methods of teaching me to read, their approach on how to create little picture books, and their intuitive instruction on how to embrace and enjoy reading as a pastime and learning tool helped me develop a true love for learning, reading, and writing—all of which became a part of my career as an author. Their education also included the joys of entertaining—teaching me how to cook, set a table, and feed people "body and soul," as Mimi said, from our tables. I will always be grateful for this education from Mama and Mimi.

Yet one teacher from high school stands out as an influence on my academic and collegiate years, as well as my career. Her name is Carol Kruger. Our families knew each other, as is the case in many small towns. However, knowing "Mrs. Carol" socially, then becoming "Mrs. Kruger's" student brought a new perspective. Mrs. Kruger taught me to love poetry, and how to respond to prose. I fell head over heels for Jane Austen under Mrs. Kruger's tutelage and learned to give myself some grace when discovering my literary voice. After all, it is MY voice, not parroting someone else's. She encouraged me to embrace my "flowery" descriptions—those descriptions now fill the pages of my books!

I remember the call from Mrs. Kruger the summer before my senior year. I had decided to leave the small school I had attended for years and enroll in the larger county high school. She was calling to welcome me to her AP English class, and to assign the summer reading list. I had to speed-read this roster to catch up with my fellow classmates, who started earlier in the summer. I read the assignments and left one title for the last conquest. I knew this book was not for me. I begrudgingly and laboriously made my way through *Pride and Prejudice*. A BBC miniseries quasi-helped me understand, but I was defeated by this novel. And to think people traveled to England just to see where Jane Austen lived and wrote; I could only imagine that to be the worst trek ever!

The Southern literary pantheon was fine by me. Some Robert Frost and Seamus Heaney poetry was perfectly lovely as well. Yet this fascination for Jane Austen that so many of the literati held caused such "solicitudes." It was just troublesome to grasp—let alone understand words such as "thither" and "vex" and "deign." Until Mrs. Kruger started her series on Jane Austen, I was lost. I was "supercilious" to become an acolyte at the Austen altar. I was "contempt" to "impute" such language into my lexicon.

And then, the parallel of familial ties, houses and gardens, holidays, and dinner parties—all set in the bucolic English countryside—began to come alive in my mind. Much akin to family dinners, garden bounties, and relationship nuances I knew as a young man from a small Southern town. Mrs. Kruger made the world of Jane Austen relatable—and then further pushed the envelope when she asked me directly, in class, if Mr. Darcy was the proud one, or was it Elizabeth Bennet who was prideful? Or was she prejudiced? Or was he? I then had to ask if I was prideful? Prejudiced? Discussions and debates about a novel from centuries before were now extemporaneous topics in our classrooms. Women's rights, social order and graces, entailments, legal standing, community involvement, and the betterment of oneself through reading, learning, and discussion were all being taught—unbeknownst to us students—through the lens of literature. Mrs. Kruger knew exactly what she was doing.

A year later, I found myself at Auburn University, taking literature classes, writing art history essays, and finding my "voice" amid my generation. Mrs. Kruger's AP English class was a genesis for sure. As I now prepare to release my tenth book, I think of how my mother helped me fold paper, staple and tape pages, and order them to create my first books. Gardening and flowers were a topic then as they are now. I can recall my grandmother loving nothing more than reading us stories and books by C. S. Lewis and performing the voices for each character. These first teachers began a good work in my love for the written word.

Mrs. Kruger instilled in me the confidence to write as a means of response—how a poem made me feel. How the relationships written in novels can be compared to friendships in my life. A threshold was crossed in her classroom. I became a Jane Austen fan. I have even been to England to see those towns and gardens that inspired her. *Sense and Sensibility* is my personal favorite. I can say confidently that learning from my pride and my own prejudices shaped me into a better person and author. Mr. Darcy, Elizabeth Bennet, and Mrs. Kruger—who knew they would have such a lasting effect on my life? Mrs. Kruger's approach was ingenious.

Julie Montagu

Entrepreneur, yoga instructor, blogger, writer,
and television personality

A good teacher makes you feel safe asking questions

My senior year of high school I had Dick Ebeling for AP chemistry, a legendary science teacher who had thinning ginger-colored hair and big 1980s glasses. I was nervous the first day of class, because he had taught my dad, who was a star student, while subjects like science and math were difficult for me. I thought, I'm going to fail this and be a disappointment to this teacher, who probably has great expectations.

I was captain of the cheerleading squad, and I wore my uniform every Friday on game day. I was the only cheerleader in AP chemistry. I felt intimidated; it was a time when the stereotype was that cheerleaders weren't supposed to be smart. The false idea that cheerleaders aren't smart started to become a strand in my life that I identified with. I was constantly worrying, Is everyone going to mock me? I had trouble meshing the two Julies: the one in the uniform who could inspire people at games, and the Julie who went to AP classes not feeling good about herself—I'm good at *this*, so why am I not good at this other thing?

Mr. Ebeling is the person who boosted my confidence in a way that other teachers couldn't. He motivated me, inspired me, stopped me from putting myself down. I used to say things like, "I'm sorry you have me in class, I'm not as smart as my brother and dad. I'm not going to be at the top of this AP class." He always made sure I was comfortable with what I was learning, but he pushed me. He taught me the skill of not being afraid to ask questions. At first it was daunting, because I'm wondering if I'm going to ask the wrong question and look dumb. But no question was dumb. He helped me reconcile the battle within myself, to realize that I could be good at multiple things. Wait, I'm just *Julie*, not Julie the cheerleader and the AP chemistry student. He helped me toss those notions away. When I went to Indiana University, Mr. Ebeling prepared me so well for the chemistry AP test that I got seven college credits before I even started school at Indiana University.

We all know teachers are underpaid. Teachers can have a massive impression on us. Children are resilient but also impressionable. The difference between a teacher and a parent is that parents tell you what you can do and what you need to do. It's more black-and-white. Teachers allow students to create their own opinions and views, and have confidence in saying, "This is what I think about this experiment." Teachers didn't always teach us about what's right and wrong, but instead encouraged us to use our voice and ask questions. When someone says, "This is what must be done, it's how it's always been done," we should ask questions. Teachers empower children, without judgment, to ask questions and solve problems. If we're silent we'll never grow or learn or become able to debate with someone. Teachers stir that up in us. Ask that question, use your voice, and learn more.

Vanessa Williams

Actress, singer

The simplest lessons can have a lifelong impact

Both of my parents were teachers. They met in the music program at SUNY Fredonia, where my dad studied instrumental music and my mom studied voice. They were both so enthusiastic about learning. If my brother or I said we didn't know what a word meant at the dinner table, we needed to go "figure it out." We'd get the dictionary and then discuss the word's meaning as a family. My mom and dad managed to find teachable moments *everywhere*.

I was fortunate to go to schools that valued and respected the arts. In fourth grade when we were studying ancient Greece, we wrote and produced a play. I can still remember the song we wrote: *Where art thou, men of Greece? Come home soon and remove our gloom!* My mom made me a toga from a bedsheet, and I danced around our version of the Trojan horse. My work on that play earned me the very long nickname Van Can Do It All Winter Spring Summer Fall. (When I ran for class president a few years later, I shortened it to Van Can Do It All, and I won!)

While I've been fortunate enough to have many great teachers, it was my high school acting teacher, Phil Stewart, who made the hugest impact on me. My high school took the theatrical productions very seriously and had an actual acting department, headed by Mr. Stewart. We had a fall play, a spring musical, a senior musical, and a spring finale (performing in the spring finale was a big deal).

My sophomore year, he gave me my first lead, in *The Madwoman of Chaillot*. He had confidence that I could deliver what the role required vocally and acting-wise. I remember how excited I was when I landed that part. I called my mom telling her I couldn't believe I got the lead! Mr. Stewart made me feel that I could do anything, from comedy to drama, and that I had the goods to make a career out of it.

It was in Mr. Stewart's class that I first learned about sense-memory work and theater games. He taught me how to break down a script. But I've carried the most important lesson he taught me throughout my entire career—show up on time and know your stuff. When I went to Syracuse to study musical theater in college, I was prepared thanks to Mr. Stewart. He taught me the vernacular, and more importantly I already knew that *preparation is paramount*! No diva behavior here!

I've kept in touch with Mr. Stewart, and he has always supported my career. He watches everything I do (and I still get critiques). When the Miss America scandal happened, I thought, Why is this happening to me? I never should have done this. No one will take me seriously. I felt like everything I had achieved had been negated by having a beauty-queen title in front of my name. I was now the "former Miss America" or the "scandalized Miss America." It was Mr. Stewart I talked to. He just said, "This is your path. These are the cards you've been given and now you just need to do your best." I trusted him that this was the right thing to do.

Mr. Stewart has taught me way beyond high school. It is so important to have dynamic teachers like him who inspire kids. Teachers mean the world for a child's development. Kids are not guaranteed a wonderful home base. Kids can be struggling with emotional distress or even violence, and their teachers can be the safe haven. Teachers mold children into the adults that they become. If they are as lucky as I was, children can learn a lesson they'll carry with them throughout their lifetime.

AFTERWORD

This is not so much a book as it is a love letter to teachers from those who cherish them. For years I basked in the glow of caring and giving educators from my childhood. I soon discovered that I wasn't alone. Anytime I mentioned a favorite teacher, someone in the conversation lit up and began sharing their own story. So it was not a complete surprise when I began thinking of collecting stories of memorable teachers that it would be one of my easiest assignments. But what *did* surprise me was how quickly anyone and everyone I approached said yes. In some cases, I happened to be talking to a friend, like Chef Daniel Boulud when I asked if he would be willing to share his memories, and before I knew it, we had an appointment to chat. The same was true with Octavia Spencer, who sent one simple text: "Sure thing." Even Lucy Liu, who was working when I reached out, days later delighted me with a response to my DM on her social media account with an emphatic "Absolutely!" People love talking about their teachers. Especially good teachers who evoke fond memories. But Lorraine Toussaint was also willing to share some painful memories of a teacher who wasn't very kind, but who helped her appreciate the one who followed and, as she says, "saved her life." Oprah so graciously didn't hesitate, either. Her brief two sentence email back to me said she is who she is because of teachers and let's talk soon. I was over the moon. This was truly a worthwhile idea! I had touched a tender spot in our consciousness. Over the years, teachers have often spent more time with us than our parents have. Their influence can be a massive moment in our lives. Many never know that they are inspiring a future CEO or an award-winning actor or a media powerhouse. Sometimes they witness this greatness in the making, and sometimes they never have an inkling of how successful a student would become. It is my hope that with this book of tributes, finally, teachers will realize what they mean to us all.

As I wrote this book, with the pandemic subsiding, I realized that I was exploring an urgent topic. Teachers, discouraged and fatigued, were leaving their profession in record numbers. Most everyone I spoke with felt saddened by this. But they also felt a responsibility to speak out and honor the work that our educators do for modest salaries. As Michael Strahan calls it, it is "the lord's work." I gathered these stories on weekend mornings, late evenings, while on summer vacation, and even while on assignment for ABC News from my hotel room. I loved every minute of the process. I came away from each interview beaming or misty-eyed about a bygone era where the teaching profession was held in the highest regard and teachers given wide latitude to shape lives and learning with their own brand of instruction. It's a different world today. We ask far more of our teachers than we ought to. Far more than what so many feel compelled to do. That is to impart wisdom, guidance, and maybe even some life lessons to our children which they will likely cherish for years to come. Let's remember that our teachers are our treasures. If you have or have had a special one, let them know what they did for you. If you can no longer reach out, find a way to honor their legacy. Understandably, many teachers aren't feeling valued these days. I hope this book is a reminder that we cherished them as much as they cherish our children.

ACKNOWLEDGMENTS

There is no way that a book like this can be written alone. While I began with a story about my own teachers from childhood, I couldn't tell the complete story of how vital they are or the dreams they have inspired without the heartfelt passion from so many others. First, I owe a major debt of gratitude to my friends, acquaintances, and the true believers who agreed to share their stories. All fifty-three of you lifted me up with your memories and your tears and your enthusiasm as you traveled down memory lane to memorialize these special souls. I still play back many of your stories in my mind daily.

But of course, this project never would've taken off without the excitement of Pilar Queen, Carole Cooper, Steve Sadicario, and the rest of Pilar's team at UTA. One meeting led to a conversation, which led to an idea, which led to a book.

I am indebted to my sunny and positive editor, Jennifer Levesque, who believed immediately in the thought of a love letter to teachers and who trusted that I could deliver it in less than a year. (Boy, was that a gutsy move for both of us!)

It's no easy feat to write a book within months. And it wouldn't have happened without the experience, creativity, and indefatigable spirit of Paula B. Vitale, who helped me turn my powerful interview material into powerful stories on the page. Thank you, Paula.

But the interviews couldn't have happened on the phone and on Zoom without Claire Lempert, a whip-smart assistant who gave up evenings, weekend mornings, and a few vacation hours to help me through the technical challenge of connecting with these busy and wonderful people who had a story to share.

Thanks to the vast team at Hyperion and Andscape Books who beamed with pride and excitement about this project—Tonya Agurto, Carol Roeder, Elias Kotsis, and Olivia Zavitson. And to Amy King and Stephanie Sumulong, who made the book a thing of beauty, and Guy Cunningham, Dan Kaufman, and Monica Vasquez, who made sure the words were something my English teacher would be proud of. Ann Day, Daneen Goodwin, Alex Serrano, and Julie Leung, I thank you for your ebullience and positive spirit about getting this book seen. And Raina Kelley, I am grateful for this opportunity to open my heart, share my love for teachers, and to write my very first solo book. I'm now an author because of all of you.

But the truth is that the wind under my wings with this project and anything else I do comes from my beautiful family. Al Roker, my husband, my cheerleader, and my touchstone, never ceases to believe in me. And my children, Courtney, Leila, and Nick have filled me with inspiration and appreciation along every step of the way with this idea, always believing that I could not only do this but would be good at it. I am humbled and heartened by your love.

And to all the teachers highlighted in this book, who are still with us or long gone, I praise your goodness, your creativity, and your hearts. You've offered gifts to some amazing people and to our world.